UTAHISMS

UNIQUE EXPRESSIONS, INVENTIONS, PLACE NAMES & MORE

DAVID ELLINGSON EDDINGTON

THE
History
PRESS

Published by The History Press
Charleston, SC
www.historypress.com

Cover photo by Bradley Morris.

First published 2022

Manufactured in the United States

ISBN 9781467152440

Library of Congress Control Number: 2022935424

Notice: The information in this book is true and complete to the best of our knowledge. It is offered without guarantee on the part of the author or The History Press. The author and The History Press disclaim all liability in connection with the use of this book.

CONTENTS

INTRODUCTION

What is it that makes Utah unique? Is it the fact that you'll find a national forest in every county or the fact that Utah is the second-driest state? Is it Utah's bizarre liquor laws or the fact that Utahns are the largest consumers of Jell-O? Maybe it's the natural beauty you'll find in the state's five national parks, five national forests, seven national monuments and two national recreation areas.

Now, if someone asks you where you *pa'ked your ca'*, you'd probably assume they are from New York or Boston, right? If they asked if *y'all want a piece of pah*, you'd peg them as a southerner. It seems that every part of the country has its own particular way of saying things, as well as words that are unique to each area, and Utah is no exception.

In this book, we'll explore the stories behind unusual Utah place names like *Tooele* and *La Verkin*, along with some Utah words and expressions that don't seem to extend beyond the boundaries of the state, like *flipper crotch* and *for cute*. Of course, many people are absolutely sure that Utahns have their own way of pronouncing words like *tour*, *mountain* and *roof*. We'll examine all of these Utahisms and more.

Besides fry sauce—a mixture of mayonnaise and ketchup—Utahns have given the world a few more substantial inventions, like video games and television. But what else can we learn about the Beehive State and what it has contributed?

There is no reason to start this book at page one. Each chapter is self-contained, so just browse the table of contents, choose a topic that piques your interest and start your journey into the fascinating study of Utahisms. I promise you that you'll be surprised.

Chapter 1

UTAH CRITTERS

Florida is famous for its manatees and California for its giant redwood trees. Now, there are a few Utah critters, but unlike manatees and redwood trees, they really haven't done much to bring fame to the state. Sometimes it is not the critter itself that is unique to a state but what it's called. For instance, most Yankees are probably clueless when they hear a southerner talking about the crawdad (crayfish) they found by the bodock (Osage orange) tree. Utah's got some unique vocabulary for some fauna, as we will see.

PANDO

Few people are aware of it, but Utah is home to the largest living being. You may think I'm referring to Sasquatch, otherwise known as Bigfoot; but no, he pales in comparison to Pando, the Trembling Giant.[1] Pando is not only enormous but also of ancient date and was already living in central Utah when the first humans migrated to the state. Pando's massive thirteen-million-pound body takes up over one hundred acres, which means that it moves ever so slowly. People travel from around the globe to visit this monster, whose color ranges from yellow to green depending on the ambient temperature. As you can guess, Pando is not your ordinary creature but a single, genetically unique aspen tree made up of over forty thousand individual trees.[2] It resides next to Fish Lake in Sevier County.

Pando. *Photo by Lance Oditt.*

POTATO BUG

In the United States, three different creatures are referred to by the name *potato bug*. One is a type of cricket (*Stenopelmatus*) also known as a *Jerusalem cricket*. The second is a type of beetle (*Leptinotarsa decemlineata*) that is often called a *Colorado potato beetle*. The third is a type of crustacean (*Armadillidiidae*) that goes by various names such as *pill bug* or *roly poly* in the United States and *wood louse* in the United Kingdom. These critters have a hard gray shell and roll into balls when disturbed. Here I am discussing the reference to these creatures as *potato bugs*.

A question in a recent dialect survey[3] asked the participants to name a picture of an *Armadillidiidae*. The results of that survey item show that these creatures are clearly known as potato bugs in Utah. This map is intriguing not because Utah is highlighted but because other small areas of Ohio and New York are highlighted as well. The Church of Jesus Christ of Latter-day Saints began in Palmyra, New York, and was officially founded in 1830 in Fayette, New York. Both of these cities fall inside potato bug zones. Religious intolerance drove members from upstate New York to Kirtland, Ohio, beginning in 1831, and northern Ohio is another potato bug area. The fact that the vast majority of English speakers in the United States uses another

Top: Jerusalem cricket. *Photo by Linda Tanner.*

Middle: Colorado potato beetle. *Photo by Sirio.*

Bottom: Potato bug. *Photo by Katia.*

term, such as *roly poly* or *pill bug*, suggests that the less common name *potato bug* may have originated in rural New York and been taken to northern Ohio with these New York immigrants. This fact could also suggest the more likely scenario that the term *potato bug* was already in use in Ohio and was the general term used along the southern shores of Lake Eerie and Lake Ontario. In either case, the distribution of *potato bug* in the United States serves as very plausible evidence that *potato bug* as a Utahism is traceable to nineteenth-century migration patterns.

Also highlighted on the map are Washington and Oregon. What about the existence of *potato bug* in these states? The Oregon Trail was the major path of immigration to the Pacific Northwest in the last half of the nineteenth century. It passed through southwest Wyoming and the Snake River Valley in Idaho, both of which are now within the potato bug zone. What is more, Salt Lake City was the only significant settlement in the region at that time. Many immigrants bound for the Northwest diverged from their path in order to take the Salt Lake/Hensley cutoff to Salt Lake City.[4] There, they would resupply with provisions and livestock before rejoining the trail and continuing their journey.

Now, taking the cutoff entailed a 360-mile detour. Is it possible that enough of the Oregon Trail pioneers took this detour and had sufficient interaction with potato bug users that they would pick up the word and carry it to the Northwest? Is it possible that the ones who didn't take the Hensley cutoff learned it from people living in the sparsely populated areas of Wyoming and Idaho? It's an interesting idea, but

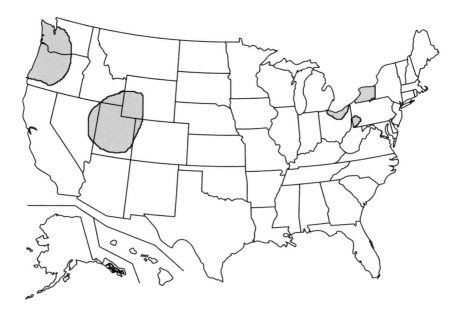

Where *Armadillidiidae* are called potato bugs. *Modified from map by Kaboom88.*

I doubt there was enough sustained contact for immigrants to pick up that vocabulary item on their way to the Northwest. Washington and Oregon were settled by people from the Midwest and New England,[5] but whether they came from potato bug areas needs to be examined in more detail before any conclusions can be reached.

POTGUT

If you hear someone mention how many *potguts* they saw while they were driving through the mountains, rest assured that this is not a derogatory reference to overweight campers. Potguts are a particular species of rodents that inhabit the Uinta Mountains of Utah and are also found in parts of Idaho, Wyoming and Montana. They are not the same thing as prairie dogs; they are potguts, although a more refined, but less frequent, term for them is *Uinta ground squirrels*, and for those of a more scientific bent they go by two names: *Urocetellus armatus* and *Spermophilus armatus*.

You can catch sight of a potgut only during certain times of the year. They awake from hibernation in the spring and then return to their underground dwellings in the late summer. During their brief appearance, they can often

Utah potgut. *Photo by Alan Schmierer.*

appear to be staging a mass invasion due to the large number of potguts that can be observed scurrying around any given mountain meadow. It is this spectacle that turns them into easy target practice for rifle-toting Utahns out on a potgut shoot.

WATER SKEETER

What makes these insects particularly fascinating is their ability to walk on water, a feat that gives them the name *Jesus bug* in some places. Biologists call them *Gerridae*, but the common folk have quite a few different terms for them: *waterbug, waterstrider, water spider, skimmer, water beetle, pond skater, water skipper, water skater* and *water skeeter*.

Where are they called water skeeters? The Harvard Dialect Survey[6] presented participants with a picture of a *Gerridae* and asked them which of five words they used to refer to this creature. *Waterbug* was the most common answer (45 percent), but 22 percent of the survey takers knew of no word for them, and 3 percent used a word other than the ones they were asked to choose from: *waterbug, backstrider, waterstrider, strider, water-spider, water crawler, skimmer* or *water beetle*. Conspicuously absent from this list is *water skeeter*. The Dialects of American English Survey[7] also included *Gerridae* as a test item, but this survey also failed to include *water skeeter* as a possible response.

How could this term not appear? I scoured billions of words in a number of massive collections of texts[8] with the grand hope of finding *water skeeter*; I found zilch. Searching the internet provided numerous references to a pontoon boat called the *Water Skeeter* that was once manufactured by a company in Stockton, California, but I found nothing that could tie the

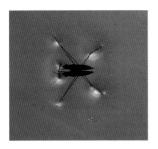

Water skeeter. *Photo by Schnobby.*

term in with the state of Utah. My suspicion—that most survey respondents who said they had another term for the bug called it a *water skeeter*—was finally verified. The Cambridge Online Survey of World Englishes[9] did include *water skeeter* as a test choice, and although the use of this term could be found scattered throughout the western United States, *water skeeter* was definitely common in Utah, which makes me conclude that *water skeeter* is definitely a Utahism.

Chapter 2

UTAH VOCABULARY
AND EXPRESSIONS

If you sit in on a conversation that turns to how people talk in Utah, you'll find that many people are absolutely convinced that the state is full of expressions that you'll never hear outside of Utah's borders. Let's take a look at some of these and see how they stack up.

CAN I HELP WHO'S NEXT?

If you've ever stood in a long line in a coffee shop, you have certainly heard the server call out to the person at the head of the line, "Can I help who's next?" The self-appointed grammar police who post online have had a heyday condemning this expression as slothful, uneducated and something that if not held in check will lead to the downfall of the English language as we know it. However, this expression is not particularly Utahn. One speculation is that it started in the upper Midwest,[10] but it's not an Americanism either because it's been heard in southern England as well.[11]

Generally, when people hear what they brand as bad grammar, they assume that it's a newfangled corruption of the proper way of speaking. That is to say, for example, they speculate that *whoever* has been shortened to *who* out of laziness. In reality, just the opposite is true. Linguists consider *who's next* an example of a fused relative construction. Fused relatives aren't new constructions; they are actually quite old and were thought to have gone extinct over one hundred years ago.[12] If you examine older documents, you'll see that *who* was used in many places where Contemporary English prefers *whoever*. Take a line from the Bard himself (that's what English majors call Shakespeare). He put these words into one of his character's mouths: "Who steals my purse steals trash."[13] Nowadays, that usage probably grates many people's ears, and most people would prefer *whoever* over *who*.

So, it seems that this old-fashioned fused relative construction didn't become altogether extinct; it somehow survived long enough to have undergone a minor renaissance, at least in the question "Can I help who's next?" In a recent survey,[14] Utahns were about equally split on whether they prefer "Can I help who's next?" or "Can I help whoever's next?" However, *whoever* was preferred a bit more by Utahns who resided in the more populated regions of the state, when compared with *who's*, which rural Utahns preferred more often.

CHURCH WORDS

In a state where about 62 percent of the inhabitants belong to the Church of Jesus Christ of Latter-day Saints (CJCLDS), you expect some church vocabulary to be part of the lingo, at least among members. I debated whether to include these terms because they are church-related rather than state-centered. That is, they are used by members throughout the English-speaking world, not just in Utah. However, as the accompanying map shows, Utah is most definitely the center of the CJCLDS population. An exhaustive list of church terms would fill an entire book, in the same way all the terms used by horse trainers, professional musicians or hackers would result in a book-length manuscript. Nevertheless, the following are some of the more common terms that those who are not members may find a bit odd.

Bishop

The word *bishop* usually conjures up images of Catholic bishops wearing long robes and big hats. Bishops in the CJCLDS, however, sport white shirts and ties as their semi-official garb. They are unpaid clergy who dedicate their "spare" time after work to ministering to the needs of a congregation.

Density of members of the Church of Jesus Christ of Latter-day Saints. *Figure by Newby.*

Deseret

Read carefully: the word *Deseret* is not *desert*, and the stress falls on the last syllable. You'll find this word in the names of Utah-centered businesses such as Deseret Industries (called D.I. by locals), Deseret Book, *Deseret News*, Deseret Trust and Deseret First Credit Union. It's a word found in the Book of Mormon and means "honeybee." The idea of industrious bees (or their beehive) as a symbol for the state made its way onto the state seal and flag, as well as into the state nickname—the Beehive State.

In 1849, two years after arriving in the region, Brigham Young, the president of the CJCLDS, envisioned a state that incorporated much of the western United States, and he suggested it be called Deseret. However, the name was much too Mormony for the higher-ups in Washington, D.C. As part of the Great Compromise of 1850, they dubbed the region Utah, after one of the predominant Native American tribes in the area, but the U.S. government wasn't ready to give it statehood quite yet. They chopped it down in size and called it Utah Territory. Another reduction in size happened in 1896, when Utah was finally granted statehood, and *Deseret* as a state name vanished into history.

Left: Utah state seal. *Figure by Svgalbertian. Right*: State of Deseret. *Figure by author.*

Deseret alphabet. *Photo by University of Deseret.*

One difficulty the Utah Territory experienced was the enormous influx of non-English-speaking settlers from places like Denmark, Wales and Germany. In 1850, about 15 percent of the population had grown up speaking a language other than English,[15] and more people from non-English-speaking countries moved in every week. Brigham Young realized that English would be the common language of the territory and wondered how all these people were going to learn to read English, with its inconsistent and messy spelling. His answer was to commission George Watt to develop a truly phonetic alphabet for English. Watt went to work, basing his alphabet on Pitman shorthand, and the result was the thirty-eight-character Deseret alphabet.[16]

Loads of money and effort were expended to teach the Deseret alphabet to the residents of Utah Territory, to print it in books and newspapers and to encourage its use. But after about twenty years, the Deseret alphabet had caught on in Utah just as much as the metric system did in the twentieth-century United States; it didn't. While Utah was isolated from the rest of the country, the Deseret alphabet may have made sense, but in 1869, the Transcontinental Railroad was completed in Utah, and all kinds of printed material, in the Latin alphabet, became readily available.

Mutual

If someone asks you if you'd like to go to Mutual, you may pause and wonder, *mutual what?* While *mutual* is an adjective for most folks, in the parlance of members of the CJCLDS, it is also a noun. It is a shortened version of the Mutual Improvement Association, which until 1974 was the name of a church organization that sponsors activities for young members. The organization was split into two separate groups and renamed the Young Men and the Young Women, but many older members still use the term *Mutual* to refer to these groups.

Primary

Primary is another one of those adjectives-turned-noun, like *mutual*. It started out as the Primary Association and was later simplified to Primary. The organization is the counterpart of Mutual, but it was designed to host activities for children between two and twelve years of age.

Recommend

English has a pattern that often allows you to tell whether a word is a verb or a noun by its stress. Take the words *implant, address* and *record*, for example. For many people, the verbs are *to implánt, to addréss* and *to recórd.* The nouns, on the other hand, are often stressed on the first syllable: an *ímplant,* an *áddress,* a *récord.* Of course, there are regional differences in how these words are stressed. For instance, in many places *cemént* is stressed on the final syllable in both the noun and the verb, while in the South, the noun is *cément.*

In general usage, *recomménd* is a verb and the corresponding noun is *recommendation.* However, in church language, the verb/noun stress pattern has been extended, resulting in the noun *récommend.* This new noun doesn't replace *recommendation;* it is a particular kind of recommendation that allows the holder access to the church's temples.

Stake

In the Old Testament, the prophet Isaiah compares the kingdom of God to a tent.[17] As God's word spreads to cover the world, the tent of His kingdom must be made larger, its cords lengthened and its stakes strengthened in order to support a larger covering. Members of the CJCLDS make use of this metaphor. When an area contains a certain number of congregations and members, an ecclesiastical unit called a *stake* is formed. This organization is usually accompanied by the edification of a new building, which in former times was called a *stake house.* You can imagine the confusion caused by the lack of steak and the abundance of cookies, punch and funeral potatoes at these stake houses. The preferred term nowadays is *stake center.*

Ward

In the United States, when local or national elections roll around, it is important to know what voting ward (or district) you live in so that you will know where to vote. When the CJCLDS was based in Nauvoo, Illinois, the boundaries of the voting wards were simultaneously used as ecclesiastical boundaries; hence, the term *ward* refers to a congregation that is determined by physical boundaries. Members attend services in the *ward* they live in rather than church-hopping to find the congregation they like the most.

CULINARY WATER

In contrast to *irrigation water*, *culinary water* is suitable for human consumption. The more common term is *potable water.* The Dictionary of Regional American English cites *culinary water* as a usage common to Utah,[18] and recent survey data[19] also support it as a Utahism. That being said, I've never had anyone from out of state slap me on the wrist for using it or make me feel that it's stigmatized. The term also appears to have escaped notice in media stories and internet discussions of what constitutes Utah English.

So, where did this term come from? Evidence suggests that it's not an Americanism. The Google Books corpus indicates the use of *culinary water* to refer to drinking water in numerous nineteenth-century British documents,[20] but the term hasn't stuck around in the United Kingdom; it appears to have fallen out of use there in the past one hundred years or so. In the United States, on the other hand, the term is still used, but principally in Utah. Why there? Well, tons of people from England immigrated to Utah in the late nineteenth and early twentieth centuries, and as a result, the influence of British English is more felt in Utah than in the rest of the country.[21] For this reason, we can probably chalk up *culinary water* as a Utahism due to English immigration.

FLIPPER CROTCH

A *flipper crotch* or *flipper crutch* is a kind of slingshot. The Dictionary of American Regional English[22] cites this term as one used in the Rocky Mountains, especially in Utah, and the evidence bears this out. Now, if you ask a Utahn what a flipper crotch is, you'll probably be met with a blank stare. Few people are familiar with this word, for two reasons. The first reason is that people nowadays just don't own, use or talk about slingshots, let alone flipper crotches. But if you are lucky enough to encounter a Utahn who does know what a flipper crotch is, chances are that they belong to the older generation. The second reason this word is unfamiliar is that the art of fabricating and using flipper crotches simply did not get passed down to the next generation, and neither did the word. Once-popular words such as *gal*, *groovy* and *swell* have suffered a similar fate with the passing of time.

FOR CUTE

I remember my cousin Nora who, when she would run across a cuddly puppy, would exclaim "Oh, for cute!" This expression probably strikes many as odd because they would feel that "Oh, how cute!" sounds more natural to them. The use of *oh for* followed by an adjective isn't limited to *cute*, either. You can also hear the interjections (oh) *for cool!*, *for gross!*, *for fun!*, *for nice!* and *for rude!*

These expressions are interesting because they are common not only in Utah but also in Minnesota.[23] What's more, they are frequent in North Dakota as well.[24] You might be thinking *what the heck?* Utah, Minnesota and North Dakota don't seem to have a lot in common. They are geographically separated, and on the surface, they don't appear to be demographic cousins. However, the key to this mysterious connection may be their shared immigration patterns.

Graham[25] suggests that the *oh, for* + adjective expression can be traced to Scandinavian languages. The map is taken from the 2000 U.S. census. It shows the distribution of Americans who claim Danish origin; Utah, southeast Idaho and a few counties in southern Minnesota are where the Danes settled in the greatest numbers. Could the *for cute* kind of interjections be due to the Danes?

Another thing that stands out on this map is the number of counties in Iowa with large Danish-descended populations. If the Danes are responsible for the *for cute* expression, why isn't it mentioned as typical in Iowa? I did an informal scour of the internet and observed quite a few *oh for* + adjective expressions used in posts related to Iowa. It appears that the use of these expressions hasn't been noticed much in Iowa yet. On the other hand, maybe the Danish connection is all wrong. On the third hand, we need to remember that this expression may also be attributed to Scandinavian influence, not just to Danish influence. While North Dakota and Minnesota may not have a huge population of Danish descendants, the number of Norwegians is huge in those states.

So the question is how to connect those three states (and perhaps Iowa as well) with two different languages. It's important to know that people in Denmark, Norway and Sweden can converse with one another without much difficulty. One Norwegian woman I spoke with confided that she often understood speakers from Sweden and Denmark better than she did the teenagers in her own country. We consider those languages to be different simply because they are spoken in distinct countries, but if history

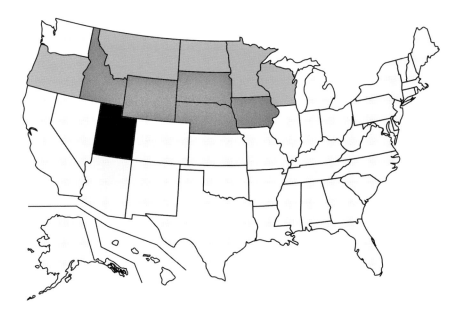

Counties with high concentrations of residents of Danish descent. *Modified from maps by Kaboom 88 and Stevey7788.*

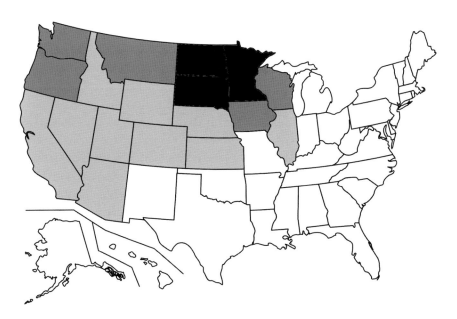

Counties with high concentrations of residents of Norwegian descent. *Modified from maps by Kaboom 88 and Stevey7788.*

had taken a different turn, in a way that those languages were spoken in the same country, we'd call them dialects of the same language rather than distinct languages.

Now, the Danes express the *for* + adjective expression in their language with *hvor* followed by an adjective: *hvor sødt!* "how cute!" and *hvor smukt!* "how beautiful!" At first glance, *hvor* doesn't look much like English *for*, but the initial two letters in *hvor* are pronounced [v], making *hvor* a kissing cousin to English *for*. As these Danish immigrants acquired English, they transferred their interjections into English, and since Danish *hvor* is English *for*, this resulted in expressions such as *for cute!* and *for beautiful!* This new construction could then spread from the Danish speakers to their English-speaking children and on to the rest of their neighbors regardless of their native language, and the expression was born.

We still need to tie North Dakota, Minnesota and Norway to all of this, which is not tough to do. *For gross* and other similar expressions in Norwegian begin with the Norwegian word *for* followed by an adjective. This means that the same expression in different parts of the United States had its genesis in two distinct, but closely related, languages.

The *oh, for cute* kind of expression appears to be on its way out in Utah. Utahns rated how likely they would be to say *for cute* or *for cool*, and most people responded that they were very unlikely to use the expressions.[26] The groups that felt they were a bit more likely to use these expressions were older Utahns, women, those who live outside the more populated areas and people who hadn't attended college. This Utahism shows all the signs of being on its deathbed.

FOR HERE OR TO GO?

When you order food at a fast-food establishment, the server needs to know whether to put your food on a tray, because you will be eating it there, or to put it in a bag because you are taking it with you. There are two common ways a server will ask about your intentions: *For here or to go?* or *To stay or to go?*

In a survey of about 100,000 Americans[27] 12 percent said they use *to stay or to go*, while the remaining 88 percent preferred *for here or to go*. In a recent survey,[28] 63 percent of the Utahns chose *for here or to go* and 37 percent *to stay or to go*. So using *to stay or to go* is definitely more common with Utahns than it is with other Americans. The phrase is preferred more by people who have spent a greater portion of their life in the state, by women, by older Utahns and by Utahns who were raised in the northern third of the state. Residents of southern Utah are more likely to use *for here or to go.*

FRY SAUCE

While ketchup is the most common condiment to dip your French fries in, Utah offers you an alternative—fry sauce. It is essentially ketchup mixed with mayonnaise, plus a few spices that are not revealed to the public. Just like the Coca-Cola people keep their ingredients secret, in Utah, the makers of each variety of fry sauce hold their recipe cards close to their chest as well.

Fry sauce. *Photo by author.*

The exact genesis of Utah fry sauce is disputed.[29] Don Carlos Edwards claims to have made it first in 1941, while Lee Porter affirms that he was the original creator in 1953. Ron Taylor and Max Peay say the year of their invention was 1955. To make matters more complex, a similar sauce, known as salsa golf, was invented in the 1920s in Argentina.[30] The inventor, Luis Federico Leloir, would go on to receive a Nobel Prize in chemistry in 1970, but not for his culinary invention.

In any event, what all of these Utah claimants have in common is a relationship to the Utah fast-food chain Arctic Circle. The spread of Utah fry sauce can be pinned on Arctic Circle, which picked up the sauce from the original inventor(s) and offered it in all of its establishments. Because of the sauce's popularity, many rival eateries devised their own versions, and fry sauce is now even available on grocery store shelves. Heinz calls its version Mayochup, something that grates on the ears of Utahns. In any event, sampling fry sauce should be on the bucket list of every visitor to Utah.

FUNERAL POTATOES

Pairing a culinary dish with death may not seem like a good way to make it sound appetizing, but that's not the source of the name. When a funeral is held in the CJCLDS, it is customary for the women's organization of the congregation to provide a meal for the family and friends. Funeral potatoes are usually on the menu. (I must admit that I was a bit put off that there were

Funeral potatoes. *Photo by GreenGlass1972.*

no funeral potatoes at my mother's funeral.) The origin of funeral potatoes is obscure, and the recipe varies,[31] but it generally consists of all the things that would uplift the grieving soul's spirits: carbohydrates and fat. The principal ingredients are potatoes, cheese, cream of chicken soup and sour cream. This mixture is topped off with bread crumbs or cornflakes and baked in an oven. Funeral potatoes are not limited to memorial events either. They often find their way into potluck dinners as well.

HOW IGNORANT!

"I can't believe they just cut in line like that. How ignorant!" In general, *ignorant* means uninformed, but a purported Utahism is the use of the word to mean rude or impolite, where it is often pronounced *ignert*. Calling the ill-mannered ignorant doesn't have Utah roots but can be traced at least as far back as to the late nineteenth century in England.[32] One common pronunciation there is *iggerant*. Referring to rude people as ignorant is still alive and well in England. I recently heard it used in a 2010 British television series[33] that portrayed a woman who didn't want to be ignorant by leaving in the middle of a friend's performance. This meaning of ignorant could definitely be another British usage that was transported by British immigrants to Utah, where it was recast as a Utahism.

I USED TO DO

Is there anything about these sentences that bothers you?

> *1a. At least I haven't heard the complaints that I used to do.*
> *2a. I think they could have done.*
> *3a. Do you want a hand, babe? I might do.*

If you are American, you probably cringe at the *do* and *done* on the end of the sentences and would prefer these instead:

> *1b. At least I haven't heard the complaints that I used to.*
> *2b. I think they could have.*
> *3b. Do you want a hand, babe? I might.*

Most British speakers, on the other hand, have no qualms about the *do* and *done*. For example, the Englishman Robert Plant croons, "I can hear it calling me the way it used to do" in Led Zeppelin's 1969 song "Babe I'm Gonna Leave You."[34] This particular use of *do* and *done* is used by the Brits much more than it is by the Yanks. It's kind of like the way Americans convalesce *in the hospital* while the British do it *in hospital*. That's not to say that you'll never hear that kind of *do* in the United States. In 1950, Hank Williams sang "Why don't you love me the way you used to do?"[35]

So, what does all of this have to do with Utah? Well, Di Paolo[36] noticed the *to do* kind of construction in the speech of Utahns and suggested that it must have been brought to the state by the myriad English immigrants who made Utah their home. In 2000, 29 percent of Utahns claimed English ancestry, which is the largest percentage of any state in the country.[37] Di Paolo also observed that the construction was accepted more by Utahns who were members of the Church of Jesus Christ of Latter-day Saints and those who were members of the Fundamentalist Church of Jesus Christ of Latter-day Saints.

Whether expressions like *he might have done* and *we used to do* are the result of English immigration, as well as whether this construction is more common in Utah than in the rest of the country, is debatable.[38] What we do know is that it has been on the decline since the state was founded. The social groups in the state that are slightly more apt to accept it are men from rural regions, older Utahns and those who did not study in college. The use of this construction depended on how much of the person's life was spent in Utah, but this interacted with religion. For practicing members of the CJCLDS, the larger the proportion of their life spent in Utah, the more accepting they were of sentences like *I used to do*. Utahns who were not members of the CJCLDS had the exact opposite trend. It looks like this grammatical construction may be a religious in-group marker, but it is one possible Utahism that the older generation may take to the grave with them.

POP OR SODA

Imagine that your friend asks you if you want a Coke and you respond, "Sure, give me a Pepsi." If your friend doesn't bat an eye and hands you a Pepsi, what part of the country are you in? You'd have to be in the South, where carbonated drinks, regardless of the label on the can, are all Coke. As the map shows, apart from the South, the rest of the country calls carbonated beverages either *soda* or *pop*.[39] Utah falls square in the *pop* region, according to this map, so you may assume that there's nothing interesting going on there, but there is.

In 1997, Lillie[40] found that *pop* was the most common term for carbonated drinks in Utah but that younger Utahns used *soda* more than older Utahns

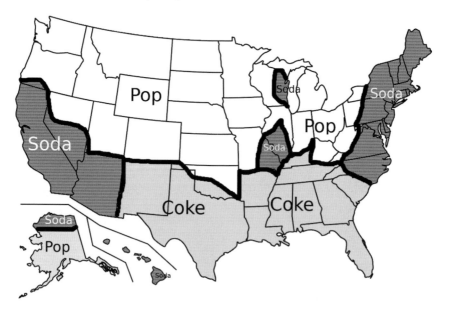

The word for "carbonated drink" by region. *Modified from map by Kaboom88.*

did. In the years since her survey was conducted, *soda* has ousted *pop* as the most common term.[41] Now, the use of *pop* is principally relegated to older Utahns, people who were raised in or reside in rural Utah and members of the CJCLDS.

SCONE

The Oxford English Dictionary[42] notes that *scone* is of Scottish origin and defines *scone* as "a large round cake made of wheat or barley-meal baked on a griddle." For most English speakers, *scone* refers to the baked variety. In the United States, this kind of bread is more likely to be called a *biscuit*. However, if you order a scone in a restaurant in Utah, what you'll get is deep-fried bread dough. There are a few other terms for this kind of food in the United States. The most general one is *fry bread*. If served with Mexican cuisine, it is a *sopaipilla*. In Native American contexts, it is *Navajo fry bread*, regardless of the tribal affiliation of the cook (and much to the chagrin of the non-Navajo cooks). The word *scone* referring to fry bread is the Utah term.

Census figures indicate that Utah's population has the highest concentration of English ancestry in the United States.[43] Given this fact, Eliason[44] suggests that it was this massive British immigration that solidly established the word *scone* in the state. Furthermore, he argues that the fried nature of the scone could be due, in part, to Utahns' contact with Mexican sopaipillas as well as Navajo fry bread. The fact that in Utah scones are fried rather than baked is most likely a matter of early frontier life, when flour and lard were staples and a frying pan was much more available than an oven.

To complicate the matter a bit, there is a hint that the fried version of the scone is not a Utah innovation after all. The Oxford English Dictionary[45] notes that one variety of scones is the fried scone, "one in which the

Left: Regular scone. *Photo by Awmalloy*. *Right*: Utah scone. *Photo by Jeffreyw*.

ingredients are made into a batter and fried." Whether the fried version was brought with the British immigrants or whether frying was a pioneer innovation, what makes scones unique in Utah, and what distinguishes them from scones in the rest of the country, is that they are deep-fried and taste so good when smothered with butter and honey. *Scone* meaning "fry bread" is the closest thing to a truly unique Utahism that there is.

SLUFF SCHOOL

Sluff, meaning "skip class,"[46] is one of the most often cited Utahisms. The alternate spelling *slough* is also cited as a Utah usage in the Dictionary of Regional American English,[47] but is this word truly limited to Utah? I searched through billions of words in online corpora for references to *sluff/ slough school* to no avail. When I googled the internet, I hit the jackpot and found numerous instances of *sluff/slough school* that were related to Utah, plus a handful of cases from neighboring states. The evidence from my searches are corroborated by the results of the Dialects of American English Survey,[48] as the map attests.[49] It's definitely looking like *sluff school* is principally a Utahism that has bled over a bit into bordering states.

Where *sluff* means "skip school." *Modified from map by Kaboom88.*

THANKS. MM-HMM, UH HUH, YOU BET

From the time you were a kid, you were taught to say *thank you* when you are given something and to say *you're welcome* if someone thanks you. My best guess is that you were not taught to say *mm-hmm* or *you bet* when you are thanked, yet those are common responses heard from many Utahns in a recent survey.[50] In that survey, 63 percent of the respondents recognized saying *mm-hmm* or *uh huh* some of the time, and 37 percent believed they never do. Younger people recognized saying *mm-hmm* or *uh huh* more than older people did.

What about *you bet*? In 1997, Lillie[51] asked Utahns how to respond to *thank you*, and 2.5 percent answered *you bet*. In my 2020 survey,[52] 62 percent of the participants responded that they sometimes use *you bet*, while 38 percent said they never do. Once again, younger people were more likely to recognize that they sometimes say *you bet* more often than older people do. *You bet* also seems to be more common in central Utah. The fact that younger Utahns are more apt to use *mm-hmm*, *uh huh* and *you bet* means that these alternates for *you're welcome* are not going anywhere and may even become more frequent Utahisms in the future.

WHAT THE HECK?

Regular old cuss words aren't as common in the Beehive State as they are in the rest of the United States. This has been proven scientifically. When you count the number of swear words in tweets and map their frequency, Utah comes out on the less vulgar side.[53] The high population of members of the Church of Jesus Christ of Latter-day Saints is surely responsible for lower rates of foulmouthedness.

The aversion to swearing among members of the CJCLDS is exemplified by the story of a young girl who stepped up to the microphone during church services and declared that her family was trying to better themselves by not saying the *s-* or *f-*words anymore. A collective gasp reverberated through the chapel as the girl's father quickly replaced his daughter at the pulpit to clarify that their family now refrains from saying *shut up* and *fart*.

Utahns' limited use of cuss words doesn't mean that smashed thumbs don't elicit verbal expletives in Utah, just that the real swear words have been somewhat modified. In Utah, the *s*-word is modified to *shiz, shoot, sheesh* and *crap*. The *f*-word, and its inflectional variants, comes out as *fetch, frickin'*, *freaking* and *flip*. Harrison[54] provides an extensive list of such terms, but a more scientific study of euphemistic swearing (used in tweets) places Utah high in the use of *crappy, dang, effing, freaking, heck* and *suck*.[55] However, the mother of all Utah euphemisms, *What the heck?*, was brought to the public's attention by Neleh Dennis, who was a contestant on the reality television program *Survivor* in 2002. She ended up winning $100,000 but was remembered more for her frequent use of *what the heck* and *oh my heck*, which garnered media attention.[56]

So, if you are peeved because you slipped in dog poop and got it all over your butt, and you yell *shoot* or *snap*, then wonder why the heck the dog's owner didn't clean up their dang dog's crap because it sucks to have to change your freaking pants, you may be a Utahn.

Euphemistic cursing. *Figure by Tomia.*

Chapter 3

UTAH PRONUNCIATION

The Bible describes a war between the Ephraimites and the Gileadites.[57] At the time of the conflict, warring factions didn't wear different uniforms and the two nations were not ethnically different, so it wasn't possible to tell the two groups apart by their appearance. However, the Gileadites knew that Ephraimites couldn't pronounce the sh sound, so when they suspected that a person was an Ephraimite, they would ask the person in question to pronounce the word shibboleth, and if that person said sibboleth rather than shibboleth, they became proverbial toast.

When people discuss Utah dialect, most of it centers not on what Utahns say but how they say it, their pronunciation. Is there anything really unique? As far as pronunciation is concerned, people tend to think that language sounds should be as solid and as immovable as a tree in the forest, when in fact, when viewed over time, the English vowels are more akin to children playing a game of musical chairs. English vowels shift one seat over, push other vowels out of the way or merge into one and the same chair. If you could go back about five hundred years, the sentence *My mate is going to boot me out of my house* would sound much more like *Me maht is going to boat may oot of me hoose*. Those particular changes are the result of the Great Vowel Shift, which affected most dialects of English to a greater or lesser extent.

It's easy to assume that the game of musical chairs stopped five hundred years ago, while in actuality it is still being played right under our noses. The vowels in the many English-speaking regions either play the shift game in their own way or don't play the same game their neighbors do. These shift games are responsible for much of the regional variation we experience today. Take, for example, the vowels in words such as *love* and *such*. At one point, these two words had the same vowel as *look* does, [ʊ]. However, in southern England, that vowel shifted into the seat occupied by [ʌ] as in *luck*, and that pronunciation was taken to the United States. Northern England and Ireland didn't play this game, which resulted in a dialectal difference: *love* as l[ʌ]ve in southern England and l[ʊ]ve in Ireland and northern England.

This kind of shifting is still taking place, even in the United States. The Northern Cities Shift[58] is what makes people from the Great Lakes region of the United States say *bad* in a way that sounds more like *bed*. Californians participate in a vowel shift that makes *friend* sound more like *frand* and *did* sound more like *dead*.[59] The vowels in Utah English have not escaped these shifts and mergers either, as we shall see. Many of the pronunciations that people assume are Utahisms have to do with the merger of different vowels into a single vowel when that vowel is followed by *l* sounds that linguists refer to as laterals. Laterals are notorious for modifying the vowels they follow.[60]

One theme that runs throughout this chapter is that most of the pronunciations that people associate with Utah are also found elsewhere. If that is the case, why do they get associated with Utah? On the one hand, it has to do with the "different means unique" phenomenon. This happens when someone travels to Utah and hears something pronounced differently from how the out-of-stater would say it. This makes them assume, often incorrectly, that since they hear it in Utah it must only exist in Utah.

On the other hand, people do comment on these pronunciations in other places. Utah's *mountain* pronunciation, for example, is commented on in the speech of Indianans.[61] In fact, pick one of the topics in this chapter and Google it and you are sure to find heated debates about who says what where and why it's wrong, weird or downright corrupted language.

Another thing that often happens is that the same pronunciation may exist in two places and go completely unnoticed in one, while in the other it is a hot topic of conversation. Why? Well, it only becomes an issue when people assign a negative stigma to it. Often, this happens when the pronunciation is more commonly used by speakers belonging to a particular social class, race, gender or region.

BOWL FIGHTING IN SPAIN

I attended a city council meeting of my small town in Utah County a few years ago. Among other items on the agenda, council members discussed a competition in the upcoming county fair in which each town would decorate a b[ʌ]l (where [ʌ] is the vowel in *but*). The b[ʌ]l from each city would be judged and the best one awarded a prize. I imagined a table covered with bowls from each city until, later on in the discussion, council members mentioned that the objects to be judged would be made of two-by-four planks of wood. How do you make a round bowl out of flat wood? I must have misunderstood, so I focused more intently on the word in question. Finally, the context of one sentence made me realize that the competition was between *bulls* made of planks, not *bowls*. In that moment, I realized that I was not the only one confused by the discussion because many members of the audience let out a collective *oh* with an accompanying shake of the head when they, too, finally caught on.

Bowl fighting. *Montage of photos by Tomas Costelazo and Coyao.*

Just how common is this pronunciation in the state? Well, Utahns were asked to match their pronunciations of the words *pull, full, wool* and *bull* with one or more of the vowels in these words: *look, Luke, lock, luck* or *bloke*. Only 31 percent matched it with the [ʊ] vowel of *look* that would indicate a general American pronunciation. The other common matches were to *luck* 24 percent, *bloke* 14 percent and *Luke* 14 percent. All of this says that [ʊ] vowels followed by laterals have shifted their pronunciation on a wide-scale level in Utah. The younger speakers and those from central Utah showed more shifting away from standard [ʊ]. This pronunciation is clearly a Utahism, but it isn't unique to the state. It is found sporadically all over the country and is very frequent in Pennsylvania and Indiana.[62]

THE CHEERLEADER'S PALM-PALMS

Discussions of grammar and pronunciation sometimes turn the most mild-mannered Dr. Jekyll into a ravenous Mr. Grammar Police Hyde. People generally assume that their pronunciation is correct and find arguments to support their assumption. For instance, some insist that the correct pronunciation of words like *palm, calm* and *caulk* is to articulate the *l*. After all, it's written in the word, right? Well, what about *walk, talk, calf* and *half*? These words are also written with an *l*, yet it's silent for many speakers. People who don't pronounce the *l* justify it because it's not pronounced in words such as *walk, talk* and *calf*, so in their view, people who do pronounce it in *palm* and *calm* are just weird and wrong.

The problem with using spelling as proof is that English spelling is far from precise. It doesn't tell you exactly how to pronounce a word; it only gives you hints about the pronunciation. There are other oddities in English spelling. For example, the silent letters in *island, debt* and *salmon* never have been pronounced, so what are they doing there? There was a time when people esteemed the art, drama and language of the Romans so much that they figured that English would be a much more elevated language if it were more like Latin. As a result, when the grammar mavens of the day encountered an English word that was similar to a Latin one (e.g., English *dette* and Latin *debitum*), they'd insert the letter from Latin into the English word (*dette > debt*). Is it any wonder English spelling is a mess?

Anyway, the written *l* in words like *palm* may or may not be pronounced in English. In Utah, people don't seem to have any negative feelings about pronouncing the *l* in these words.[63] I asked Utahns to tell me whether word

Cheerleader's palm palms. *Montage of photo by Mike Morbeck and Timothy A. Gonsalves.*

pairs like *pom/palm* and *stalk/stock* were pronounced the same. In 60 percent of the responses, the pairs were judged as different, which I take to mean that *l* was pronounced.[64] Pronouncing *l* was more prevalent among the college educated, older speakers and residents of the more populated regions. It was less common among nonpracticing members of the CJCLDS. Before deeming it a Utahism, it would be nice to see how frequently *l* is pronounced in these words in the other forty-nine states.

THE FISH IN THE CRICK

I've heard some people say that a sure way to tell if someone is from Utah is if they pronounce *creek* as if it rhymed with *stick* with the [ɪ] vowel instead of the [i] vowel in *peak*. If that were true, then Tom Sawyer would have been a Utahn. Mark Twain put these words in his character's Missouri mouth: "Just as I was passing a place where a kind of a cowpath crossed the crick, here comes a couple of men tearing up the path as tight as they could foot it."[65] I hate to break it to those people, but that particular pronunciation was actually found all across the United States in one recent dialect survey.[66]

The pronunciation of *creek* in Utah has drawn attention for quite a while. In Lillie's study,[67] 31.4 percent of her participants said *cr*[ɪ]*ck* and 61.1 percent *cr*[i]*ck*. The *cr*[ɪ]*ck* pronunciation was more common in the older respondents and in speakers from the central part of the state, followed by speakers from the southern portion. It was least frequent in the north.

I'm sure there are language purists who insist that the proper pronunciation of *creek* has to be *cr*[i]*ck* since the double *ee* spelling in English gives us *feet*, *sweet* and *keep* with the vowel [i], which no one would pronounce with the vowel [ɪ] as if they were *fit*, *swit* or *kip*. Unfortunately, the English spelling system is notoriously inexact, which makes appeals to spelling quite shaky. I'll simply cite the word *been*, which no American who wasn't trying on a British accent for effect would ever pronounce in the same way as *bean*. *Been* is normally pronounced *bin* [bɪn] or *ben* [bɛn] in the United States, just like creek often is.

What may add to the purists' horror is that even the esteemed Merriam Webster Dictionary can't help but cite *cr*[ɪ]*ck* as a pronunciation of *creek*.[68] It's important to realize that dictionaries simply document what the speakers of a language say. Dictionary compilers don't invent words or pronunciations to grace the pages of their volumes and then insist that those words or pronunciations be used by English speakers. The written word has always been based on the spoken word, not vice versa. It is clear that *cr*[ɪ]*ck*, while common in Utah, is common elsewhere, and this disqualifies it from being an exclusive Utahism.

THE GOLF OF MEXICO

Pronounce these words and pay attention to how you say the *u*: *hull*, *gulf*, *cult*, *result*, *ultimate*. Now say these words and focus on the *u*: *putt*, *luck*, *rut*, *bump*. One common pronunciation is to say all of the *u* vowels in the same way, [ʌ] as in *up*, but if you are like many Americans, you probably pronounce the *u* vowel differently in the first group because it is followed by an *l* sound. As I mentioned earlier, linguists have observed that *l* sounds tend to modify the vowels that precede them so that they merge with another

Golf of Mexico. *Modified from figure by Apuldram.*

vowel. This often causes these pairs of words to be pronounced the same: *hall/hull, golf/gulf, cult/colt.*

To see what's going on in Utah, I asked survey takers to match the vowel in the words *dull, pulse, pulp* and *gulf* with the vowel in one or more of these words: *look, Luke, lock, luck, bloke.*[69] Wow, did they give me a variety of responses. They matched the words with the vowel in *luck* in 48 percent of the cases, but other responses included 15 percent that were matched to *bloke*, 14 percent to *look*, 7 percent to *Luke* and the rest matched to more than one vowel.

So who matched more of the words with a vowel other than [ʌ] (as in *up*)? It looks like the move away from [ʌ] is championed by women, younger Utahns, those who were born and raised in the state and nonparticipating members of the CJCLDS.

THE HARSES IN THE BORN

When I moved back to Utah after living in a number of other states for fourteen years, I announced to friends and colleagues that I had found a home in Spanish Fork. "Spanish Fark, eh? I heard that the Marmons warship the Lard there. How harrible!" Yep, this is one of the most talked about, stereotyped and stigmatized features of Utah English. It's called the *cord/card* merger because it makes pairs of words like these almost identical: *born/barn, four/far* and *pour/par.*

You are probably guessing by now that this merger is not unique to Utah, and you'd be right. In the United States, the *cord/card* merger is concentrated in parts of Texas and St. Louis.[70] In one survey,[71] the pronunciation of *Florida* yielded many cases of vowels other than [o] in *Florida* scattered throughout the country, particularly in the Northeast and South.

Pardoe[72] thinks that immigrants from the Northeast are responsible for the existence of the *cord/card* merger in Utah, and I think he may be onto something. Think about where people who talk about the *Part Autharity* or the *Flarida Arange Bowl* are from, and the Northeast comes to mind. A lot of northeastern immigrants came to Utah in its early days. In fact, in 1880, 26 percent of the U.S.-born residents of Utah hailed from New York, Pennsylvania or Massachusetts.[73]

Genetic testing has also confirmed the strong ties between Utah and the Northeast. One of the companies that promotes genetic testing,

Genetic relationships according to Ancestry.com. *Modified from map by Kaboom88.*

Ancestry, sorted through the DNA of its clients, grouped people with similar genetic characteristics together and then plotted them on a map.[74] In general, genetically similar people tend to live in the same geographical area. However, one of Ancestry's groups was widely separated. Ancestry's denomination for this group is the Northeast and Utah. In a court of law, this kind of evidence would not constitute definitive proof, but it sure makes you suspect that northeasterners brought the *cord/card* merger to Utah.

Given all the hype surrounding the *cord/card* merger, you'd think you'd hear it a lot more than you do. What's happened is that in the early twentieth century, most Utahns ate *carn* and tied up their *harses* with a *card*,[75] but Utahns who were born after about 1950[76] started eating *corn* and didn't have as many *horses* by then and the older pronunciation started being associated with rural, less educated speakers.[77] It's gotten to the point that you're really only going to hear the *cord/card* merger from Utahns with more than seven decades under their belt, so while it may have been a Utahism, it's not going to last much longer if this downward trend continues.

HE FELLED THE TEST

One college student from Utah was asked what his career plans were, to which he responded that he was going into *cells*. The person who inquired assumed that this was an unusual way to say he was going to be a biologist, but further questioning revealed that he intended to be a salesman; he was going into *sales*. This is an example of the *fail/fell* merger. It is one of the top pronunciations that people cue in on to distinguish Utahns,[78] but does that mean that when one crosses from Wendover, Nevada, into Wendover, Utah, suddenly everyone goes to the post office to get their *mel* if it's *avelable*? No, variation in pronunciation just doesn't work that way. It depends on social factors. For example, Lillie[79] found the *fail/fell* merger to be more frequent among central Utahns, younger speakers and the less educated, while Sarver[80] observed it more among men and rural residents. In Utah County, this merger was more prevalent among members of the CJCLDS.[81]

What complicates the matter is that the *fail/fell* merger isn't uniquely Utahn. I found *for sell* in eighteen of the twenty English-speaking countries represented in a large international corpus,[82] and it has been documented all over the United States as well.[83] So, if you hear someone say that they *felled* a test, don't be 100 percent sure that they are from Utah.

He felled the test. *Photo by author.*

HOW DO YOU FILL?

A robber walked into a café in Salt Lake City, handed the cashier a bag and told the cashier to fill it.[84] The cashier complied with his demand by reaching out and feeling the bag. Frustrated, the robber replied, "You've got to be kidding," and left. The would-be holdup was thwarted by what linguists call the *fill/feel* merger. The two vowels we are talking about are the vowels in *feet* and *fit*. Of course, no one would confuse these words and say something like "Are your shoes hurting your fit?" The merger happens only when the vowels appear before *l* sounds, and I've already mentioned that there is something about *l* sounds that makes the vowels before them harder to distinguish. Such is the case in word pairs such as *feel/fill*, *seal/sill*, *steel/still* and *peel/pill*.

The *fill/feel* merger is one of the things that people most strongly associate with a Utah dialect,[85] but it's far from unique to the mountains, valleys and deserts of Utah. You'll find it in Texas and in the South, as well as scattered all over the country.[86] In Utah, it's more common in the speech of the less educated, younger speakers and central Utahns,[87] as well as people who have lived a larger proportion of their life in the state.[88] In one study, people who merge these vowels were viewed as less friendly and less educated.[89] So, while this merger is clearly a Utahism, it's not a characteristic that is unique to the Beehive State.

I'M DAWN, NOT DON

In the nineteenth century, people in search of land, religious freedom and gold flocked to the West from many different eastern and midwestern states, as well as from various English-speaking countries. In the West, the dialects spoken by the native-English-speaking immigrants met the nonnative accents spoken by the Greeks, Chinese, Italians and Scandinavians, and in the course of just a few generations, all of those different varieties of English coalesced into the western dialects we now have.

When a new dialect is formed under conditions of massive dialect contact, the result tends to be a kind of simplification called dialect leveling.[90] As an example, consider the words *Mary*, *merry* and *marry*. In some dialects, each of these words is pronounced with a different vowel sound. In other varieties of English, only two are pronounced identically, while in many dialects, all three are pronounced the same. In the West, the two- or three-way distinction that existed in the speech of some settlers was leveled to no distinction at all in the newly formed dialects, making *Mary*, *merry* and *marry* homophones. This is dialect leveling.

Now consider the words *Don* and *Dawn*. If you pronounce *Don* and *Dawn* the same, you use the vowel [ɑ] for both, but in many English dialects, the two words have different vowels; *Don* has [ɑ], and *Dawn* has [ɔ]. (If you don't distinguish the two and need help wrapping your head around what [ɔ] sounds like, think about how a British person pronounces the vowels in *dog* or *all*.) In dialects that distinguish *dawn*, *caught*, *bought*, *walk* and *stalk*, all contain [ɔ], while *Don*, *cot*, *bot*, *wok* and *stock* have [ɑ]. In the western United States, [ɔ] has generally been merged with [ɑ].[91]

So, what's the deal in Utah? Well, Utahns born between 1847 and 1896 merged these vowel sounds at a rate of about 60 percent,[92] but speakers born later merged them more, and the merger has continued to dominate until the present day. Along with other westerners, most Utahns don't distinguish between [ɑ] and [ɔ]. However, the situation is a bit more complex because, although Utahns claim to say words like *caught* and *cot* the same way and don't perceive a difference in how they sound, when you examine Utahns' pronunciations acoustically, there are subtle differences.[93] For example, older speakers from Utah County merged more than younger speakers did,[94] which is odd because you'd expect the older speakers to retain the distinction more.

As far as religion is concerned, people from Utah County merged the [ɔ] and [ɑ] sounds to the same degree regardless of their religion,[95] but when their speech was examined acoustically, the exact vowel that [ɑ] and [ɔ] had coalesced into was slightly different between the non-CJCLDS, practicing CJCLDS and nonpracticing CJCLDS groups. For example, the nonpracticing CJCLDS group pronounced the vowels with a lower tongue position than practicing members did.

Utahns, for the most part, have eliminated the contrasting [ɔ] vowel from their speech, just like most westerners have. They also feel that people who don't use [ɔ] sound more prestigious.[96]

I SPELLED MELK ON MY PELLOW

Got melk? Is your pellow too hard? I've often heard these pronunciations pawned off as a sure way to spot a Utahn. Of course, these pronunciations will often fall from the lips of Utahns, but they are far from unique to the state of Utah; they are actually quite common around the Great Lakes,[97] in California[98] and in parts of Canada.[99] In Utah, the older folks and those from the central and southern parts of the state are a bit more likely to say *pellow* and *melk*.[100] So, I hate to break it to you, but *melk* and *pellow* are poor yardsticks for classifying a speaker as hailing from Utah or not.

LAURA

Is *Laura* pronounced *Lara* or *Lora*? In Utah, 72 percent felt that *Laura*, *Lauren*, *laurel* and *Lawrence* matched the [ɑ] vowel in *lawn* rather than the [o] vowel in *loan*,[101] the [o] being another common pronunciation. In a previous section, "The Harses in the Born," I discussed how older generations of Utahns merged [o] into [ɑ] in words like *cord* and *fork*, resulting in *card* and *fark*. The *cord/card* merger is generally relegated to the older generations of Utahns, and it's rare to find a younger speaker talking about how the army used *harses* in *Warld Wahr I*. I believe that the *Laura* as *Lara* pronunciation is related to that dying process but didn't bounce back to [o]. Let me explain why.

The *cord/card* merger originally resulted in an [ɑ] vowel in words like *corn*, *horse* and *warm*, pronounced as *c*[ɑ]*rn*, *h*[ɑ]*rse* and *w*[ɑ]*rm*. It often gave the [ɑ] vowel to *Laura*, *Lauren*, *laurel* and *Lawrence*. When parents christen their child *Lauren*, *Lawrence*, *Laura* or *Laurel*, they attach a pronunciation to that name. That is fine for *Lauras* with [ɑ], but it sometimes means that *Lauras* with [o] may go through their lives telling new acquaintances that it's *L*[o]*ra* not *L*[ɑ]*ra*. When the *cord/card* merger was common, *Laura* with [ɑ] dominated, and since people don't like to change how their name is said, the pronunciation of proper nouns like *Laura* essentially rendered them immune to change. So even while the *cord/card* merger was dying out, the [ɑ] vowel in these names resisted shifting into [o].

Nevertheless, the pronunciation of names like *Laura* does vary in Utah.[102] The [ɑ] vowel is more common in certain counties, among older Utahns and among practicing members of the CJCLDS. In Utah, *L*[ɑ]*ra* is the most frequent pronunciation of *Laura* and similar words, but whether Utah is unique in this regard requires data on the pronunciation of speakers from other states for comparison.

MY PLAYSURE

Having grown up in the CJCLDS, I was accustomed to listening to the discourses of church leaders on television. When they spoke of *treasures in heaven*, *earthly pleasures* or the *measure of a man*, I was always struck by the way these septuagenarians and octogenarians pronounced the words *measure*, *pleasure* and *treasure* with the [eɪ] vowel in *late* instead of the [ɛ] vowel as in *let*. I just chalked it up as an old man thing.

Now it must exist beyond the boundaries of Utah because the Merriam Webster dictionary gives both *m*[eɪ]*sure* and *m*[ɛ]*sure* as pronunciations.[103] Internet discussions of the topic suggest that the Midwest is the focal point of -[eɪ]*sure*, and many online discussions make it clear that people who use -[eɪ]*sure* are stigmatized or made fun of. Savage found that among Utahns, the pronunciation is associated with less friendly speakers.[104]

In a recent survey,[105] only 11 percent of the responses to *measure*, *treasure* and *pleasure* were -[eɪ]*sure*, and this pronunciation was more frequent among older Utahans and those who live, or were raised, outside the more populated regions. The fact that this pronunciation is common in the Midwest makes me wonder if Utah's founding settlers, many of whom had lived in Ohio, Missouri and Illinois, are the source of this pronunciation in Utah.

ODD GO IF AH HAD MONEY

Is Utah English influenced by southern dialects? There is one trait that Utah may share with the South, which is the pronunciation of words such as *tie*, *pie* and *I* as a single vowel [a] (think of a southern accent) rather than as the diphthong [aɪ]. I'm skeptical that this pronunciation was brought to the state from the South, however. In his study of recordings of Utahns who had been born in the nineteenth century, Bowie[106] observed that in cases where the diphthong [aɪ] was possible, 16 percent were pronounced as a simple [a]. This pronunciation was more common in the speech of those born later in the nineteenth century. However, in the early twentieth century, the [a] pronunciation started its decline.[107] It had been more common in the Salt Lake Valley than in southern Utah. In turn, speakers from southern Utah showed more evidence of the pronunciation than speakers from Utah and Cache Counties did.

The great majority of the cases in the studies I have mentioned consisted of the pronoun *I* and contractions like *I'd*, *I'll*, *I'm*. The problem with the focus on *I* is that really common words and expressions undergo phonetic reduction. An example of phonetic reduction occurs with the phrase *I don't know*. It's so frequent that it gets reduced to *I dunno* or even to something like *uh-ah-oh*. So maybe the apparent shift from [aɪ] to [a] is actually phonetic reduction, making *I'd go* sound more like *odd go*.

In any event, the existence of [a] instead of [aɪ] persists into the twenty-first century. Sykes[108] documents it in the speech of seven Salt Lake City residents; the men produced more cases of [a] than the women did. Sykes's study was not limited to *I* and its contractions, however. Sarver[109] examined the pronunciation of the word *tie* and found that 30 percent of all cases were [a], and for the participants ages fifty-five and older, this rose to 60 percent. In another study of Utah County residents,[110] all cases of [aɪ] were found to be diphthongs. However, when the exact nature of the diphthongs was examined acoustically, the researchers observed that the practicing members of the CJCLDS produced the glide of the diphthong (i.e., the [ɪ] part) with the tongue raised significantly higher in the mouth than the nonpracticing members of the CJCLDS did.

THE PRINTS OF WALES

Have you ever heard people insert a [t] in the middle of words like *also* or *answer*, making them into *altso* and *antswer*? I've run across lots of people who decry these kinds of insertions as terrible, horrible English. Being the inquisitive linguist that I am, I ask them why it's bad. They invariably resort to spelling as their evidence: "It's incorrect to pronounce things that aren't in the spelling." If that is true, wouldn't it also be incorrect to not pronounce letters in a word? That idea makes perfect sense to them until I point out words such as *castle* and *hasten*, in which the *t* isn't pronounced. "Well, that's different," they respond.

Some people assume that sloppy speakers just grab some random consonant and throw it into words for no apparent reason. The truth is that the inserted consonants are never random; they are actually quite predictable. The inserted consonant is one that naturally transitions from one sound to another. For example, the [t] in *also* makes a nice transition from [l] to [s], something that [p] or [k] just wouldn't do. Consider the words *assumption* and *consumption*, which are related to *assume* and *consume*, not *assumpe* or *consumpe*. In these words, we actually write the transitional inserted [p]. Although we often add a [p] to *hamster* (*hampster*) in the exact same way, we haven't yet gotten around to allowing the inserted consonant into formal spelling.

Many other inserted consonants also serve this transitional role. The [k] in *strengkth* is an example, and adding these kinds of consonants isn't just something that happens in contemporary English, either. If we went back in time, we'd see *thimle*, *bramle* and *pumkin*. Speakers inserted consonants in these words so often that the new consonant came to be represented in the spelling: *thimble*, *bramble*, *pumpkin*.

Unlike other inserted [t]s, the pronounced word-final [t] in *acrosst* can't be explained as transitioning between consonants. It has been around since at least the eighteenth century[111] and is well attested to on the East Coast.[112] Could it be due to the similarity between *across* and *crossed*? Remember that the final -d in *crossed* is pronounced [t]. In any event, although many of these inserted consonants make linguistic sense, people have a pretty negative view of them.[113]

In one study,[114] six of fourteen Utahns produced one of the test words, such as *faltse*, at least once, with an intrusive [t]. However, it seems that people don't think highly of this pronunciation. Speakers who use it are perceived to be less friendly.[115] In a survey, I gave Utahns words like *also*, *Celsius* and *Hansen* and asked them whether they pronounced the words with or without an intrusive [t];[116] 24 percent of them recognized that they insert the consonant in at least one of the test words. Younger speakers and those raised outside the more populated regions did slightly more insertions. I'll classify this as a Utahism, but once again I'd really like to see how frequently [t] gets inserted in words of this sort in other parts of the country.

ROOF

For many people, *roof* rhymes with *proof* with the [u] vowel, and some claim that only Utahns fail to rhyme *roof* and *proof*, instead giving *roof* the [ʊ] vowel that *would* has. The evidence for the correct pronunciation, they claim, is in the spelling; all these words with *oo* are pronounced with [u]: *spoof*, *aloof*, *food*, *choose*, *moon*, *shoot*, *google*, *mood* and so on. So, *roof* needs to follow suit.

Now while I don't dispute that those words have the same vowel, I merely point out the messiness of English spelling that does things like put seemingly random letters in words that no one in their right mind would ever pronounce. Consider the *s* in *island*, the *w* in *sword*, the *t* in *castle* and the *gh* in *fight*, *caught* and *though*, to mention a few. Evidence from English spelling is so fluffy that it would certainly never hold up in a court of law. The truth is that most letters have several pronunciations in English. Take the letter *a*, for instance. It rolls off the tongue in a different way in *last*, *taste*, *large* and *allow*. The same is true for *oo*. It is a written representation of the [u] vowel in *proof* and *moon*, but it is also used to represent the [o] sound: *floor*, *door*. To make matters even more confusing, *oo* is also used to write the [ʊ] sound in words such as *good*, *took*, *hook*, *brook*, *soot*, *foot*, *book* and, for many people, *roof* as well.

On a map of the United States, it's actually next to impossible to find a dividing line that shows where *roof* is pronounced *r*[u]*f* and where it's *r*[ʊ]*f*.[117] In a recent survey, *r*[ʊ]*f* was seen to be well established in the

Midwest.[118] In a 2020 survey of Utahns, 20 percent favored r[ʊ]f, and this pronunciation was more common among older Utahns and those raised outside the more populated regions.[119]

The first takeaway from this fact is that you shouldn't look to *roof* when you're trying to find a unique Utah pronunciation. The second is that perhaps Utah got this pronunciation from the Midwest. In the nineteenth century, members of the CJCLDS spent a great deal of time in Illinois, Missouri and Ohio before fleeing to the Rocky Mountains. They may have packed r[ʊ]f in their wagons and handcarts alongside their other supplies.

STICKING PENS AND WRITING PINS

If you ask someone in the South for a *pen* or *pin*, they may ask for clarification: "Do you want a writing pin or a sticking pin?" In many parts of the United States, the [ɪ] vowel as in *pit* and the [ɛ] vowel as in *pet* become merged when they appear before nasal sounds like *n*. Now Utah is far from the South, but this merger is often brought up in discussions of Utah English, even though the vast majority of Utahns keep *pen* and *pin* distinct.[120] Only 13 percent of Utahns merged the vowels in a recent study, and this tendency was a bit more prevalent among those who had not attended college, those who were raised or reside outside the more populated regions and those who were not members of the CJCLDS.[121] I'm going to have to classify this one as not really playing any part in Utah speech.

SUNDEE SCHOOL

I was always perplexed by my parents' and grandparents' pronunciation of the days of the week ending in *-dee* instead of *-day*. I never heard younger people talking about going out on *Saturdee*. Then, one day I caught myself saying *Sundee shoes*. I certainly never called the day of the week *Sundee*. Maybe I belong to the group that falls between the old-timers and young-uns, for whom the *-dee* pronunciation is kept only when the day of the week is used as an adjective, as in *Sundee school* and *Sundee shoes*.

In 2020, only 4 percent of the Utahns surveyed reported the *-dee* pronunciation in their own speech.[122] I was positive that age would influence it, but no cigar. Vaux and Golder, on the other hand, found this pronunciation scattered throughout the entire country.[123] So when you hear someone talking about their plans for *Fridee*, don't count on them being from Utah.

THE SWIMMING PULL

Those dang [l] sounds are once again wreaking havoc on the poor vowels that come before them. In the case of *pull/pool*, what we have is the [u] vowel in *Luke* turning into the [ʊ] vowel in *look*, but only before [l] sounds. This means that the underlined vowels in the sentence *the cool rule the pool in high school* can vary between [u] and [ʊ]. People who merge the two vowels will say *fool* and *full* the same way and *pool* and *pull* with the same pronunciation. This tendency gives this phenomenon the name the *pool/pull* merger.

Of course, this vowel merger exists in Utah,[124] but it has also been observed beyond the boundaries of the state. It is found sporadically around the United States but is quite frequent in Pennsylvania and Indiana.[125] In a survey conducted in Utah in 1997,[126] 21.5 percent of the participants

The swimming pull. *Montage with modified photo by Grundarfjörður.*

pronounced *pool* as *p*[ʊ]*l*, and the older group used this pronunciation more often. In contrast, in a 2004 study, the younger speakers merged [u] and [ʊ] to a greater extent.[127] In a 2020 survey,[128] Utahns matched words like *cool* and *rule* with the [u] vowel in 62 percent of the cases and to [ʊ] in 23 percent. The other 15 percent were matched to other vowels or combinations of vowels. Preferring [ʊ] was more frequent among younger Utahns, those with less education, those who live or were raised outside the more populated areas and those who are not members of the CJCLDS. Pronouncing words like *school* and *rule* with the [ʊ] vowel instead of [u] is extremely common in Utah, but the question that remains is how this pronunciation in Utah compares to that in other states.

TOUR

When I was in high school, I was told that my pronunciation of *tour*, the one that rhymes with *core* with an [o] vowel, was very typical for a Utahn. That puzzled me because I knew words spelled with *o-u-r* like *four* and *pour* that no one in their right mind would pronounce as *foor* or *poor* with the [u] vowel, and Seymour the Cat was definitely called *Seymore*, not *Seymoor*. Despite all of this, when I moved out of state, I caved to linguistic prejudice and consciously changed my pronunciation to *t*[u]*r*.

But, you are asking, that is the common pronunciation in Utah, right? Well, in Lillie's survey[129] it was about half and half: 55 percent *t*[u]*r* and 45 percent *t*[o]*r*. Now, there are a good number of people who are convinced that there's something wrong with *t*[o]*r*, and that pronunciation raises lots of eyebrows in internet discussion groups, but the discussions are not just about its use in Utah. When I searched the internet, I found the *tour* rhyming with *core* pronunciation discussed in the speech of people from New Jersey, Ohio, California, New York, the East Coast and Canada, which leads me to be fairly confident that it's not unique to Utah. The Cambridge Dictionary cites *t*[u]*r* as the American pronunciation and *t*[u]-*uh* as British.[130] This is similar to the entry in the Oxford Learners Dictionaries,[131] except that this dictionary gives the word a second British pronunciation—*t*[o]*r*, where the final *r* is optional, of course. As I've discussed in previous sections, Utah became the home of many British people, and that makes me very suspicious that they may have been responsible for introducing or solidifying *t*[o]*r* in the state.

The participants in a recent study were asked how they pronounced *tour*, and once again, they split 52 percent *t*[o]*r* and 48 percent *t*[u]*r*.[132] *Tor* was a bit more frequent for participants who had spent a higher percent of their life in the state, as well as for younger Utahns, members of the CJCLDS and folks from central Utah. So this one is a Utahism but not a unique Utahism.

UTAH'S MOUN'UNS

"Utahns say *mountain* weird." After returning to Utah following a fourteen-year stint in other states, I heard this sentiment expressed quite often. When I pressed people on what they meant by "weird," they responded that Utahns drop the *t* in *mountain*. Some refer to this tendency as *t* dropping, and it makes me shudder every time I hear that term, especially in the news, because if the *t* were erased from *mountain* it would sound like *moun*, and it doesn't. What is really going on is that the pronunciation of *t* has shifted to a glottal stop, which linguists write with this funky character: [ʔ]. I know you're thinking, "What the heck is a glottal stop?" Glottal stops are very common in American English. Try saying *Batman plays football.* Unless you are speaking ultra-slowly or with a British twang, the sentence will come out *Ba*[ʔ]*man plays foo*[ʔ]*ball.*

So there is no *t* dropping in words like *mountain*; it's *t* glottalization, but even that's not unique to Utah. In casual speech throughout the United States, the standard pronunciation of *mountain* has a glottal stop—that's how John Denver sang "Rocky Mountain High." "OK," you may say, "but there is still something about the way Utahns pronounce *mountain.*" Yes there is, but it really has nothing to do with the *t*. What people are actually cuing into is what they hear after the glottal stop. You've built up pressure while pronouncing the glottal stop, and you need to release it. If you channel the released air through your nose, you get an [n], resulting in the general American pronunciation *moun*[ʔ]*n*. This is a nasal release. However, if you release the air through your mouth, instead of getting an [n] right after the glottal stop you produce a vowel before the [n], resulting in *moun*[ʔ]*uhn*. I call this an oral release, and this is the Utah pronunciation that people are talking about. It occurs in lots of words, like *curtain*, *eaten*, *fountain*, *button* and *Layton.*

So who does it? We asked Utahns to read a passage containing a number of words like *tighten* and *button*, and in 17 percent of the cases we registered an oral release pronunciation.[133] The highest use of oral releases was among young females who had spent most of their life in the state. In another study, it was exclusively the Utah women who produced oral releases.[134]

Because people in Utah make so many negative comments about oral releases, they have a negative stigma attached to them. This was measured in an experiment by Savage,[135] who played a series of audio recordings to listeners. The recordings were essentially identical except that in one case there was an oral release and in another a nasal release. The listeners were asked to judge the speakers they heard on a number of personality traits. Speakers whose recorded speech contained oral releases were judged to be less friendly and less educated than those who used nasal releases. We got similar results in a separate study.[136] In addition to being judged as less friendly and less educated, people who spoke with oral releases were also viewed as more rural.

So, many Utahns use oral releases, but are oral releases exclusively Utahn? Nope. They've been heard in other states like California, Vermont, Connecticut and New York.[137] They've also been discussed and parodied in a number of internet discussions about the speech of New Mexicans and Indianans. Earl Brown and I observed oral releases in 24 percent of the *mountain*-type words we studied in New Mexico, 12 percent in Utah, 9 percent in Indiana and 2 percent in Mississippi.[138] So while oral releases are definitely a Utahism, they aren't exclusive to the state either.

Chapter 4

UTAH PLACE NAMES

From *Mexican Hat*, *Koosharem* and *Kolob* to *Ripgut Creek* and *Shivwits*, Utah has its fair share of unusual place names. Heck, it was hard to decide what to include here. This chapter contains just a smattering of what you'll find in the Beehive State, and if you're in the mood for more information about place names after going through this chapter, take a look at Van Cott's[139] extensive treatment of the topic.

BEAVER

Yep, it was named after the beavers found in the area. Nope, there is no movement to get it renamed, unlike what happened to Beaver College in Pennsylvania, which changed its name to Arcadia University due to the infelicitous connotations with the word *beaver*.[140] Beaver has a few claims to fame. It won a contest for the world's best-tasting water,[141] and it is the birthplace of the inventor of television, Philo Farnsworth. Not everything is rosy in Beaver, however; it is also the hometown of the infamous Butch Cassidy.

BIRDSEYE

I was once told the family that started the Birds Eye food company was from Birdseye—not true. The community is named after the birdseye

Above: Beaver. *Photo by Peeweejd.*

Left: Birdseye marble. *Photo by James St. John.*

marble mined from the nearby quarries.[142] Much to the chagrin of Birdseye residents, the most well-known person from their community is Shawn Nelson, who was born in Birdseye. In 1995, Nelson stole a tank—yes, a real tank—from an armory in San Diego and went on a spree that included smashing or damaging forty cars, along with light posts and numerous fire hydrants, before being shot by police.[143]

CALLAO

The tiny desert town of Callao was named by a nineteenth-century prospector in the area who thought it looked like Callao, Peru.[144] While both cities may fall in deserts, I'm wondering how much whiskey the old prospector had imbibed when making this comparison. Unlike the Callao in Utah, the Callao in Peru is situated next to an ocean, has palm trees and enjoys a moderate climate. While in Peru the pronunciation of Callao is something like *kah-yao*, it's nothing like the Utah pronunciation, *cal-ee-o*. The word derives from Portuguese and means "rocky beach."

DUCHESNE

There is both a county and town named Duchesne. Let's get the pronunciation of *Duchesne* out of the way here. It's not *doo-chess-knee* or *duchess*. It's *doo-shane*, which makes it suspiciously French. Was it named after someone or something French? Well, the two facts we have about the name are that Duchesne is a French surname, and it is similar to other French names. We also know that French trappers worked the area around the Duchesne River. Those two facts seem to have been the basis of a bunch of unsubstantiated theories about the origin.[145] Maybe it was named after a trapper named Du Chesne, or maybe a trapper named it in honor of Mother Rose Philippine Duchesne, a French nun who founded a number of Catholic schools in frontier America, or after the French historian André Duchesne. The word itself means "of the oak tree."

But wait; the city falls into Ute territory, so there is speculation that it was named after an unidentified Ute chief. Some suggest that the name is derived from Ute words meaning "dark canyon," but Dirk Elzinga, a specialist in the languages of the state, tells me that "dark canyon" is highly suspicious etymology. When it comes down to it, we really have no idea where Duchesne got its name.

Nevertheless, Duchesne County produced a few names that people may recognize. Evan Mecham was born in Duchesne County and went on to become governor of Arizona from 1987 to 1988; however, he was impeached and removed from office for misuse of funds. Laraine Day, born Laraine Johnson in Roosevelt, Utah, was a Hollywood actress with a career that spanned from the 1930s into the 1980s. She acted alongside the likes of Robert Mitchum and Gregory Peck. She also authored a number

Laraine Day. *Photo by Studio Publicity.*

of books about baseball. You can find her star on the Hollywood Walk of Fame. You may not have heard of Walter Frederick Morrison, who was born in Roosevelt in 1920, but you have surely played with the Frisbee he invented.

DUTCH JOHN

They got the name of Dutch John all wrong. After John Honselena migrated to Utah, he made a living as a horse trader and miner. He was a German speaker who evidently had quite a thick accent. When a new town was established in the area where he used to keep his horses, the founders honored him by dubbing the town Dutch John;[146] however, John was not Dutch.

Here's the problem. People from the Netherlands are Dutch and speak Dutch. On the other hand, people from Germany obviously speak German, but they call their language *Deustch*, which sounds a lot like *Dutch*, hence the confusion. This isn't the first time this mix-up has happened. You've

Flaming Gorge. *Photo by Frans-Anja Mulder.*

probably heard of the Pennsylvania Dutch. Just like John, they were actually German, not Dutch.

While Dutch John may not sound like the kind of place that anyone would go out of their way to visit, it actually is that type of place. Nearby Flaming Gorge is a popular vacation spot that offers rafting, fishing, camping, boating and water skiing.

HELPER

Helper was originally a railroad town called Pratt's Landing.[147] It lies at 5,817 feet above sea level, and the westward-bound trains had a steep climb of 1,660 feet ahead of them to get to Soldier Summit, which is only 23 miles away. To make this climb possible, additional engines, called helper engines, were added to the trains, hence the name. Once the trains reached Soldier Summit, the extra engines were removed and then coasted back to Helper. Robert Mullins, who won a Pulitzer Prize in 1962, grew up in Helper, as did Helen Papanikolas (b. 1917), who wrote extensively on the experience of immigrants in the West.

Helper. *Photo by Loco Steve.*

HOOPER

Two things make Hooper unique. First, it is the only Utah city with an island in its boundaries. Yep, Hooper reaches into the Great Salt Lake to include Fremont Island. The other point of interest is its name. On the face of it, *Hooper* doesn't seem like a noteworthy town name, but what makes it unusual is its pronunciation. People know in a second if you are not from Hooper if you mispronounce it. The locals pronounce the *oo* as it's pronounced in *look* and *book*, not like the *oo* in *boot* or *raccoon*.[148] The town was named in honor of Congressman William H. Hooper, and he pronounced his own name that way, so there.

This pronunciation isn't unique to Utah, however. Both the vowel in *look* and the vowel in *boot* are cited as pronunciations of the first vowel in the word *hooper*.[149] If you happen to travel to Hooper, Nebraska, residents there will also tell you it's *Hooper*, like *hooker*, but with a *p*.

HURRICANE

The saying "When there's a will, there's a way" is aptly applied to Hurricane, at least as far as its canal is concerned. The need for water in a desert climate like Hurricane's led to an ambitious project started in 1891.[150] The daunting task of routing water through the area's sandstone canyons and cliffs made most deem the project impossible, but not James Jepson and John Steele, who led the enterprising settlers in constructing a 7.5-mile canal to divert water from the Virgin River to their lands. That 7.5 miles may not sound like a big deal if you live in Kansas, but the settlers had to blast twelve tunnels through the red-rock country to build the canal. In some places, they even had to hang the canal on the side of the cliffs. It was completed in 1904 and allows Hurricane to exist in the Utah desert.

Given Hurricane's dry climate and landlocked location in Utah's southern region, one wonders how it got its name to begin with. According to town history, in 1896, a gust of wind caught Erastus Snow by surprise when it blew the top off his buggy. The force of the gust was so hurricane-like to him that Erastus christened the nearby prominent point Hurricane Hill, after which the town was subsequently named.[151]

Another intriguing question is why the residents of the town pronounce it *Hurri-kun* rather than the more common *Hurri-cane*. The unique pronunciation of the town name serves to distinguish the locals from the

Above: Fremont Island.
Photo by Gene Selkov.

Right: Hurricane Canal.
Photo by Jack E. Boucher.

outsiders. This kind of linguistic group marking is actually quite a common phenomenon. New Yorkers, for example, are more likely to pronounce *Manhattan* as *Mun-hattan* rather than *Man-hattan*. Similarly, residents of Prescott, Arizona, rhyme their hometown with *biscuit* rather than pronounce it *press-cot*. In Utah, outsiders who are aware of how native Hurricanites refer to their town have been known to snicker at the unusual pronunciation, but interestingly, the residents' supposedly idiosyncratic, novel or, heaven forbid, corrupted pronunciation is actually not unique at all.

The Cambridge Dictionary lists both American and British versions of *hurricane*.[152] The American pronunciation is *hurri-cane*, while the British pronunciation is *hurri-kun*, so the question isn't why the pronunciation was altered in southern Utah but how a Britishism made its way into the Utah desert. Now, most of the early settlers of Hurricane came from other parts of Utah,[153] so that isn't very telling. However, Utah was swamped by immigrants from Britain, who made it the state with the highest concentration of British ancestry in the country.[154] Those immigrants didn't simply drop their speech patterns as they got off the boat in the United States; they brought their old-world pronunciations, along with their genetic material, to the Beehive State. *Hurricane* may have been one of the things that they brought with them.

LA VERKIN

Because *La* is separated from *Verkin*, you may think that *La Verkin* is of Spanish origin. Perhaps the name is an anglicization of Spanish *la virgen*. After all, the Virgin River does border the town. There are two problems with that theory, however. First, the Virgin River was named after Thomas Virgin, who was an explorer in the area. Second, the earlier Spanish explorers Domínguez and Escalate named the river *Río Sulfureo* in reference to its hot springs, so no cigar.[155]

The stream that hedges in the city of La Verkin on its west side is La Verkin Creek. In early documents, this creek is referred to by a number of names: *Levier Skin*, *Leaverskin*, *Levier Skin*, *Leaversking* and *Laviskind*.[156] All of these appear to be variants of *beaver skin*, perhaps because the letters *l* and *b* could be confused in the handwriting of the day. You may be skeptical that *b* and *l* could be mistaken for each other, but the way *b* was written in nineteenth-century U.S. script made it easy to confuse with *li* and *le*.[157] All the good evidence supports the theory that *La Verkin* derives its name from *beaver skin*.

La Verkin Creek. *Photo by Aoiaio.*

LEVAN

The running joke is that since Levan falls square in the middle of the state, it was jocularly named *navel* spelled backward. However, Arave[158] points out that when the town was named in 1868, the modern borders of the state of Utah hadn't yet been determined, and the center point of Utah Territory would have fallen somewhere closer to the Nevada border town of Ibapah.

The messiness of figuring out where a place name comes from is exemplified by Van Cott.[159] He states that the name *Levan* could derive from Latin, French or Paiute and mean either "east of the sunrise," "land of the sunrise," "rear rank of a moving army," "frontier settlement" or "little water." Van Cott's claim leaves you trying to search for five terms in three languages. For example, is "frontier settlement" a French, Latin or Paiute word?

The idea that Brigham Young named the town *Levan* because it means "rear rank of a moving army" suggests that *levan* is a Latin word. I doubt Brigham Young knew French or Latin, let alone Paiute. Even if he did, such a specific term would not have been likely to grace the pages of a nineteenth-

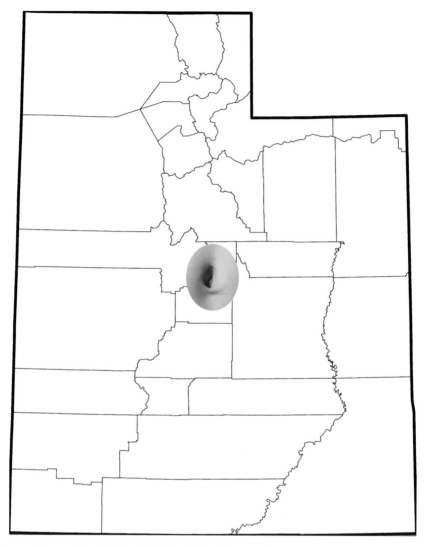

Levan. *Montage of modified photo by Tbiggs1995 and figure by David Benbennick.*

century French or Latin book. In reality, I can't find anything remotely similar to *levan* as an army term in French or Latin, and I'd like to know if there is actually a word for "rear rank of a moving army" in English. The word doesn't seem to relate to any of those meanings in Paiute, either. In my book, the actual origin of *Levan* is a mystery. The pronunciation of *Levan* also lets people know if you are from that part of the state or not. Outsiders say *la-ván*, but true Levanites (or Levaners) know it rhymes with *seven.*

MANTUA

The little town of Mantua, with a population under one thousand, sits on the banks of a reservoir surrounded by mountains and seems almost idyllic. There aren't many income-generating businesses in town, so it has garnered a reputation as the biggest speed trap in the state. In 2018, the number of speeding tickets given out by Mantua police officers exceeded the number of town residents,[160] and in 1997, half of the revenue the town generated was in the form of speeding-ticket income.[161]

You may think the name of this lakeside town is of Native American origin, but it isn't. What makes the name especially unusual is its pronunciation. It's not *man-two-uh* but *man-away*. Where on earth did the Utah residents come up with that? It turns out they didn't. The town was actually named after Mantua, Ohio, where CJCLDS leader Lorenzo Snow was born, and guess what? *Man-away* is how the Ohioans pronounce it. *Mantua* follows a common pronunciation process in American English. Think of words like *winter*, *twenty*, *Santa* and *county*. In casual speech, the *t* isn't pronounced in these words, nor is it pronounced in *Mantua*. In any event, the town of Mantua, Ohio, got its name from the Italian city of Mantua.

The town of Mantua, Utah, United States, as seen from U.S. Route 91. *Photo by Ntsimp.*

SANPETE, SANTAQUIN AND JUAB

Surely the place names of Sanpete, Santaquin and Juab are Spanish in origin. They look like modifications or bad spellings of something more Iberian like *San Pete*, *Santa Quín* and *Juan*—except that they aren't. Come on, *San Pedro*, yes; *San Pete*, no. They are actually all Native American words. The Sanpitch River and mountains were named after a band of Utes or their leader.[162] *Sanpitch* means "people of the tules."[163] The river and mountains still bear this name, but it was modified into *Sanpete*, which is the name of the valley and county. *Juab* is also of Native American origin; it means "flat or level plain."[164] By the way, it's pronounced *jew-ab*, not like Spanish *Juan* with a *b* substituted in.

Santaquin was possibly the name of a Ute chief.[165] However, local history tells a different story:[166] the town got its name from a would-be Native American warrior. Here's how it played out. The area that would become the town of Santaquin was settled in 1851, and a fort was constructed there. Soon after, war broke out between the Native Americans and the white settlers. Although the war was over by 1856, the bitter feelings it caused still festered.

Sanpete County and Sanpitch Mountains. *Photo by C. Maylett.*

64

A local Native American, Chief Guffich, had become friends with the settlers. One day, he heard that some of his people planned to attack the settlers in the fort and that his son was among the planners. I imagine that the horrors of the recent war were fresh in his mind, along with the fact that he did not want to be caught in the middle of a fight between his people and his newfound friends. To thwart the attempt, Chief Guffich warned the settlers, who fled the fort. When the assailants arrived, there was simply no one in the fort to attack. When the factions made peace, the settlers wanted to name the town after Chief Guffich for his role in keeping them from being another casualty of war, but Chief Guffich declined and suggested that they instead name the town in honor of his would-be warrior son, Santaquin.

SPANISH FORK AND AMERICAN FORK

A person from out of state who is traveling through Utah County is sure to wonder what nationalities and silverware have to do with the towns of Spanish Fork and American Fork. Is there a German Spoon or a Chinese Knife nearby as well? The truth is that both American Fork and Spanish Fork were named after the rivers that run through them, and it is tempting to interpret *fork* to mean a fork in the river. However, the Spanish Fork and American Fork rivers are not branches, tributaries or forks of another river.

So how did these towns get their names, and what does *fork* mean? The word *fork* is related to the most salient feature of the state of Utah, which is its mountains. The landscape of a mountain is composed of higher portions called *peaks*, *ridges* and *crests*, while the lower parts are known as *canyons*, *ravines*, *gulches* and *draws*. In Utah, these depressed areas in a mountain were also called *forks*, and in Utah, as well as in other parts of the West, this name was applied regardless of whether a river ran through the area or not.

The name *Spanish Fork* may give one the impression that the town was settled by the Spanish, but in reality, the largest group of early settlers was Icelanders,[167] a fact that residents celebrate with a monument and a festival. The *Spanish* part of *Spanish Fork* refers to the 1776 expedition undertaken by a party of Spanish explorers led by fathers Francisco Atanasio Domínguez and Silvestre Vélez de Escalante.[168] The expedition set out from Santa Fe in search of a route to Monterey, California, and one stretch of the explorers' journey took them along what is now known as the Spanish Fork River, named in their honor and named before the Icelanders arrived.

Festival of Colors in Spanish Fork. *Photo by Steven Gerner.*

In addition to the town's ties to Iceland and Spain, Spanish Fork is known for the Sri Radha Krishna temple, where a Hindu Festival of Colors is hosted. The festival draws over forty thousand people to the temple grounds each year.[169] After reciting the names of the Hindu god Krishna, festival participants shower one another with brightly colored powders made of cornstarch.

The town of American Fork was of course named after the American Fork River. One theory about how *American* became attached to the river name is that it was derived from the American Fur Company, whose mountain men trapped beaver along the river. Another theory is that the river was dubbed the American Fork simply to distinguish it from Spanish Fork, which is found farther to the south.[170]

Famous Spanish Forkers include Lucky Blue Smith, a well-known male model, and the Candy Bomber, Gail Halvorsen, who during the Berlin blockade rained candy down on the children of East Berlin. Fantasy author Brandon Sanderson hails from American Fork, as do two members of the band Imagine Dragons, Daniel Wayne Sermon and Andrew Tolman.

ST. GEORGE

What do Nebraska, the Utah desert, scurvy and a cold winter have in common? St. George, Utah, of course! What? To understand this, let's take a step back in time to Illinois in the year 1847. Members of the Church of Jesus Christ of Latter-day Saints had built a large city in Illinois, second only to Chicago at the time, but had been facing persecution there. They'd already been kicked out of New York, Ohio and Missouri. Having appealed to the governor of Illinois and the president of the United States with no luck, they were planning on leaving the country behind for good and heading to Mexico in the spring, but the escalating violence, barn burnings and political pressure forced them to cross the frozen Mississippi River to the Nebraska side starting in February of that year.

They set up a shanty town in Winter Quarters and hunkered down to wait out the rest of the winter before pushing west. However, the conditions in Winter Quarters were bleak. Soon, lack of proper nutrition reared its head in the form of scurvy. People's limbs turned black and bled. Their gums swelled up, and their teeth fell out. Hundreds died.

George A. Smith, although not a medical doctor by any means, had the simple cure: one merely had to eat unpeeled potatoes. He may have learned of this while serving as a church missionary in England or through correspondence with members in Britain. In any event, he distributed potatoes to those that he could and preached the doctrine of eating unpeeled potatoes as a means of lifting the scourge to the rest. Many in the camp recovered as a result of his efforts.[171]

Once established in what would become the state of Utah, many members were assigned to settle different parts of the western United States, as well as parts of Mexico and Canada. George was the church leader who chose the first company of settlers who were sent to southern Utah in 1861. The idea was that the more temperate climate there would be ideal for cotton cultivation. George himself never established residence in the southern part of the state that came to be known as Utah's Dixie (a moniker that is currently trying to be eradicated).

Potato saint. *Montage of modified photo by Zoofari and figure by themidnyteryder83.*

Unlike Catholics, who bestow the title of saint on particularly godly men and women or on those who have performed noteworthy feats, members of the CJCLDS generally use the term *saint* merely to refer to a follower of Christ (e.g. Ephesians 1:1). Nevertheless, those settlers dubbed the town they founded St. George[172] in honor of what "Potato Saint George" had done fourteen years earlier on the cold, wintery plains of Nebraska.

TIMPANOGOS

My mother was wrong. I only discovered this when I was in my fifties. As a kid, whenever we'd travel on the far side of Utah Lake, she would direct my attention to the mountain on the other side of the lake and point out how it looked like a woman asleep on her back. "*Timpanogos* means sleeping maiden," she would tell me. I forgive her because even Encyclopedia Britannica got it wrong, citing "reclining woman" as the translation.[173]

The word *Timpanogos* is Ute and means "water flowing over the rocks." The name was probably first applied to the Provo River and then to the mountain by extension.[174] When the Spanish explorers Domínguez and Escalante arrived in Utah County, they called the mountain *La Sierra Blanca*

Mount Timpanogos. *Photo by A4gpa.*

de los Timpanogotzis, "the white mountain range of the Timpanogotzis," after the Timpanogotzi band of Utes that lived in the valley.[175] Many local businesses and groups use the abbreviated form, *Timp*, in their appellations: Timp Books, Timp Rentals, Timp Archers, Timp Valley Floral.

TOOELE

A man was traveling from California on I-80 and had just driven through the Bonneville Salt Flats. Feeling hungry, he took an exit into a place that looked like it would offer a variety of fast-food chain eateries. As he exited the freeway, he noticed the strange name of the town he had just pulled into: *Tooele*. He found a fast-food restaurant and placed his order. As he was eating, an employee asked him how his meal was. "Fine," he answered, "but I do have a question. How do you pronounce the name of this place?" With a puzzled look on her face, and with careful articulation, she answered, "Bur-ger-King." Perhaps the man wouldn't have been so perplexed if he saw the older spelling of the area—*Tuilla*. *Tooele* is not pronounced *tool-y* or *two-el* but *two-ill-uh*.

So where did this name come from? There are numerous theories, most of which can be easily dismissed. The first Europeans to set eyes on Utah County were Atanasio Domínguez and Silvestre Vélez de Escalante.[176] On September 23, 1776, they arrived in present-day Spanish Fork. Escalante was born in northern Spain, in the town of Treceño. The first theory is that the Tooele area reminded Escalante of the town of Tuilla, Spain, and so he dubbed the area *Tuilla*. There are three problems with this theory. The first is that Tuilla, Spain, lies about eighty-seven miles from Escalante's hometown. Was he familiar with that town? Well, he was born around 1750 but migrated to Mexico, where he became a Franciscan friar at the age of seventeen, so he spent only his early childhood in Spain, and it is unlikely that he could have traveled enough in his native country to have been familiar with Tuilla.

The second difficulty with this theory is that the farthest north his expedition took Escalante was Spanish Fork. Tooele lies fifty-nine miles northwest of Spanish Fork, so he never set eyes on the place, let alone gave it the name. Third, how could anyone equate an area of the Great Basin desert with a town in the lush, verdant mountains of Spain's Asturias?

A number of other theories have been put forward.[177] One is that the valley was "too hilly" or was "too willy," meaning there were too many willows.

The area is both flat and too arid to support an abundance of willows. There are, however, bulrushes called *tules* that grow in the swampy areas, and some people have speculated that the plant's name got mispronounced into *Tooele*. Another theory is that Orson Pratt named the place after a town he had visited in the Austro-Hungarian Empire, Mattuglie. However, Pratt visited it twenty years after Tooele was named.

So what's the real story? The name *Tooele* most likely comes from a family of Indigenous people belonging to the Goshute tribe, who inhabited the valley. The family name was Tu-Wada, which in the Goshute language sounds a bit more like *two-ill-uh* to English ears. And what exactly does the word mean? Black bear.

UTAH

There's nothing mysterious about the name Utah. It obviously comes from the Utes who lived there, right? Well, no. First of all, *Utah* is not a Ute word at all. The Utes call themselves *Noochee*, meaning "people." Another idea is that *Utah* means "the top of the mountains." This etymology is a folk legend propagated by members of the CJCLDS to relate their temple in Salt Lake City to Isaiah 2:2: "And it shall come to pass in the last days, that the mountain of the Lord's house shall be established in the top of the mountains, and shall be exalted above the hills; and all nations shall flow unto it." (KJV)

We do know that *Utah* comes from the Spanish, who used the word *yuta* to refer to the inhabitants of the region. But how did the Spanish come by the word *yuta*? One theory is that *yuta* is the word the Pueblo people used to refer to the Utes. Another is that *yuta* (and later Utah) comes from the Apache word *yuttahih*, which is what the Apaches called the Navajos. It means something like "one who is higher up" or "the people up there." The Spanish may have misunderstood that the name *yuttahih* referred to the Navajos and applied it to the Utes instead.[178]

It may seem counterintuitive to call a people, or their country, by a name other than the name they call themselves, but we do it all the time. The country we call Germany is known by the Germans as *Deutschland*, and its inhabitants are the *Deutsch*. The Finns call their country *Suomi*, not Finland. For the natives of Egypt, their country is *Al-Misr*, and so on. If, by some fluke of history, we had named the Beehive State correctly, it would have been known as the state of Noochee, not Utah.

Delicate Arch. *Photo by National Park Service.*

THE Y AND THE U

If you are completely clueless about what the Y and the U are, then you are most definitely not a Utahn. They are the nicknames for Brigham Young University and the University of Utah, the second- and third-largest universities in the state. What? Yep, in 2020, Utah Valley University had 40,936 students, the Y had 35,615 and the U had 33,080. The university nicknames come from the large block letters plastered on the mountains close to each campus.

The history behind both mountainside letters began in the 1900s, when the tradition at both schools was for seniors to use lime to paint their graduation year on the mountain. The University of Utah halted this tradition in 1907 when the school decided to place a permanent U there rather than having the hillside change every year.

The decision to install a permanent Y was not so peaceful. In 1906, the juniors at Brigham Young High School, the precursor to Brigham Young University, decided to one-up the seniors and painted their graduation year,

The Y. *Photo by Arbyreed.*

The U. *Photo by Scott Catron.*

07, on the mountain before the seniors got a chance to paint their 06. This, of course, enraged the seniors, who marched up the mountain, confronted the juniors who were left to guard their class symbol, expelled them from the site and then angrily erased the blasphemous 07. The seniors' wrath didn't stop there. Offending juniors were captured and had their heads shaved as punishment.[179] It was this scandal that prompted the administration to install the Y. The original plan was to spell out BYU. They started with the middle letter Y, but given the enormity of the task, they forwent the B and the U. Had they started with B, BYU's nickname would have followed, and BYU would have been known as the B instead of the Y.

At first, the U and the Y were made of rocks and needed to be repaired and whitened by the students each year. The present U is made of concrete and stands 100 feet tall. It is located 1,074 feet above the valley floor and is equipped with red and white lights. When a University of Utah sports team wins a game, this news is broadcast to the valley by a U that flashes red and white.[180]

The Y is 380 feet tall and is located about 1,600 feet above the campus. It is composed of cement-covered rocks and is lit for events like homecoming and graduations. The fierce rivalry between the two schools has at times included painting the letters with the school colors of the opposing university, but these supposed acts of school spirit have become less frequent since many of the more recent perpetrators have faced criminal charges of vandalism.

Among the many notable alumni from the U we find J. Willard Marriott, founder of the Marriott Hotel chain; Martha Raddatz of ABC News; and Republican politician Karl Rove. The Y boasts presidential candidate Mitt Romney; Philo Farnsworth, the inventor of electronic television; and fantasy author Stephenie Meyer. Science fiction author Orson Scott Card attended both universities.

Chapter 5

OTHER UTAH STUFF

DEPARTMENT STORE

The world's first department store was born out of xenophobia and religious persecution, really. Members of the CJCLDS in the nineteenth century had been driven from state to state and attacked by mobs and armies. They'd finally had enough, so they removed themselves from what was then the United States and settled in the Rocky Mountain wilderness. However, persecution didn't end when they arrived in the Salt Lake Valley, which only solidified their fear, distrust and suspicion of anyone who was not of their faith.

By the late 1800s, the us-versus-them mentality was deeply entrenched in the state's inhabitants. Further complicating the issue was that many church members were wary of doing business with one another for fear that their prosperity could be seen as taking advantage of others or that it could put them in the uncomfortable situation of having delinquent loans owed to them by other church members.[181] In spite of the mistrust they had for nonmembers, a great deal of church members' business transactions were done with those who were not members.

The nonmember business owners were accused of charging higher prices to members. This alleged practice, when coupled with the large number of nonmembers who began to flood the territory in 1869 when the railroad arrived, prompted the members of the CJCLDS to turn inward and solidify their position against the influences of those who did not belong to their

ZCMI Department Store. *Photo by Tamanoeconomico.*

faith. In the financial sphere, this turning inward led to the formation of the Zion's Cooperative Mercantile Institution (ZCMI) in 1869.[182]

Basically, anything that could be made or grown, including food and livestock, was traded at ZCMI, and the first department store was born. The idea behind this church-owned business was self-sufficiency. The market was to be composed principally of locally made goods—in other words, goods made by church members—and the items were to be sold to other members at prices lower than they were offered in nonmember businesses. The faithfulness of members who chose to trade outside this co-op was suspect, and some were excommunicated from the church for such violations. ZCMI actually printed its own kind of money for in-store transactions, known as ZCMI script. Of course, this led to large losses by many nonmember businesses.[183]

Over time, the CJCLDS loosened up restrictions, and ZCMI became a publicly traded business open to all. It eventually turned into a swanky operation with stores in many western states and with ties to the likes of *Seventeen* and *Glamour* magazines.[184] In 1999, it was sold to May Department Stores and closed its doors.

FEMALE SENATOR

Martha Hughes Cannon.
Public domain.

Martha Hughes Cannon was the first female state senator in the United States.[185] Cannon was an immigrant from Wales who heard Brigham Young encourage women to become physicians, so she took him up on it and received her MD from the University of Michigan in 1880. She became the fifth of the six wives of Angus Cannon in 1884, just six years before the CJCLDS ceased practicing plural marriage. However, at that time the government was actively prosecuting polygamists, so Martha exiled herself to Europe for a few years to avoid testifying against her husband.

Women in Utah had been given the right to vote in 1870, but in 1887, the U.S. government revoked their right in Utah,[186] so Martha threw her efforts in with other women's suffrage activists like Susan B. Anthony to fight for voting rights to be restored to Utah women and to be extended to women in the rest of the country.

In 1896, Cannon ran for the Utah state senate as a Democrat and won. It was an important milestone for women's rights in U.S. politics, but it was noteworthy in another regard as well. You see, the Republican candidate that Martha beat in the election was none other than Angus Cannon, her husband.

FRISBEE

What if you could buy something in the store, walk a few blocks away and sell it for five times what you bought it for? Great business model, right? That's what Walter Frederick Morrison, of Roosevelt, Utah, thought. His family had moved to California in the 1930s, and he and his girlfriend, Lu, had become really adept at tossing a pie pan to each other, Frisbee style. One day, an observer saw them having fun with the pie pan on the beach and offered to buy it from them for twenty-five cents. Hey, the pan was only five cents in the store, and thus was born the business idea.[187]

Over the years, Morrison and his friend Warren Franscioni improved on the pan design and made it of plastic. When they sold the rights to

Frisbee. *Photo by Marco Consani.*

the flying disk to Wham-o in 1957, it was called the Pluto Platter, but somewhere along the lines the disk-flipping customers started referring to the saucer as a Frisbee, and the name stuck.

JEWISH GOVERNOR

Not only is Utah the state with the most members of the CJCLDS, but with the exception of Wyoming, Utah is also the most Republican state in the Union. In spite of these demographics, in 1917, Utahns chose Simon Bamberger to be their fourth governor. Bamberger was not only the first Democrat to hold that office in the state, but he was also Jewish. (Later on, in 1925, Utahns elected George Dern, another Democrat who was not a member of the CJCLDS.) Bamberger could be considered the Andrew Carnegie of Utah. Simon and his brother Jacob were German immigrants who started on the bottom and worked their way to the top. Their mining ventures made them both a fortune. Simon invested much of his wealth in railroads and other businesses in the state. In 1896, he established an amusement park halfway between his railroad line from Salt Lake City to Ogden. To this day, it still carries its original name: Lagoon.

Left: Simon Bamberger. *Photo by Harris & Ewing.*

Below: Lagoon Amusement Park. *Photo from Boston Public Library Tichnor Brothers collection.*

KENTUCKY FRIED CHICKEN

KFC is from Utah? What the heck? What about Colonel Sanders? To understand the history of Kentucky Fried Chicken, you have to go back to Indiana in 1890, when Harland Sanders was born.[188] Sanders did serve in the military, but he never got close to the rank of colonel. That title was bestowed on him by the State of Kentucky as an award given to outstanding citizens of Kentucky, kind of like how the queen of England knights people, but not nearly as posh.

The Colonel owned a gas station in Corbin, Kentucky, called Sander's Court and Café. He called his gas station a café because he sold fried chicken and other food out of it. When Sanders perfected his fried chicken recipe, he realized that it had great potential, and he decided to franchise the recipe. That way, he could earn a commission on each piece of chicken the franchises sold, and he wouldn't have to do the cooking and selling himself. The first entrepreneur to see the potential of the chicken recipe, and the first one to buy a franchise, was Pete Harman, a restaurant owner in Salt Lake City. Pete ended up owning a few hundred KFCs. According to my family history, my grandmother Nora Eddington, who worked for Pete, was asked by Pete to join him as a partner in this new business venture. She turned the opportunity down, citing her need to spend her time raising her children.

Kentucky Fried Chicken. *Photo by Wierse.*

When the time came for Pete to name the new restaurant, he and his sign painter, Don Anderson, almost named it Utah Fried Chicken, but they didn't like the sound of it. Because Sanders was from Kentucky, and because Kentucky conjured up the idea of southern hospitality, what got painted on that first building was Kentucky Fried Chicken, and thus KFC was born.[189]

79

LIQUOR LAWS

You can't get a cold beer in Utah, right? Wrong. Nine states in the Union have dry counties, but Utah isn't one of them.[190] The drinking age in Utah is twenty-one, and beer is available in grocery stores, but only beer with 4 percent alcohol by weight or less. Utah is one of seventeen states where the state has a monopoly on liquor sales,[191] and in Utah, anything stronger than 4 percent is considered liquor. As such, it must be purchased in a state-run liquor store or one of its licensed package agencies. Those agencies are mainly found in resorts and hotels. If you want to drink in Utah, be sure to stock up before the weekend, because the liquor stores are all closed on Sunday. You'll also need to get 'er done early, since no drinks are served after 1:00 a.m.

Utah recently lowered the legal blood alcohol level that is considered drunk driving to 0.05 percent. This contrasts with the rest of the country, where it's 0.08 percent. Back in 1983, Utah dropped the legal limit from 0.10 percent to 0.08 percent, which caused quite a stir at first. It took a while, but in 2000, Congress made the rest of the country follow Utah's lead and lowered the limit nationwide to 0.08 percent. The National Transportation

Utah liquor laws. *Photo by Prayitno.*

Safety Board had been calling for a 0.05 percent or lower limit long before Utah actually implemented it.[192]

One peculiarity in the state is that if you want to order a drink in a restaurant, you are required to order some food to go along with it.[193] That's what separates a restaurant from a bar, according to state law. And in a restaurant that serves alcohol, the drink itself must be prepared at least ten feet away from the prying eyes of any minor, although minors are free to observe adults actually drinking. That requirement is actually a softening of the law in effect prior to 2017. Back then, the drink preparation had to be concealed with a partition of some sort, affectionately known as a "Zion's curtain."

Liquor laws in Utah have loosened up quite a bit, and much of what was bizarre has been legislated away. For example, it used to be that it wasn't just the liquor stores that were closed on Sunday. Open grocery stores couldn't sell beer on the Sabbath either. Before 2002, you had to pay a membership fee to join a club before buying a drink in a bar. As far as home brewing is concerned, each adult is allowed to produce one hundred gallons of beer, cider or wine, but nothing stronger. However, you can only remove seventy-two ounces of it from your home at a time so that you can't be considered a distributor.[194]

NAMES IN UTAH

You can tell you're from Utah if you are Brayden, you mother is Sariah and your grandparents are Alma and LaRue. Or can you? Utahns have a reputation for carrying unusual names.[195] Many older residents of the state have names beginning with *La-* or *Le-*, such as LaNae or LaVelle. One study that compared Utah and Colorado baby names from 1982, 1990 and 1998 found converted surnames to be prevalent in Utah, such as Dustin, Colton, Skyler, Tyler and Colby for boys and Whitney, Haley, Courtney, Mackenzie, McKenna and Madison for girls.[196] That study noted that, for a while, the fashion was to give boys names with two syllables ending in *n*: Braxton, Brayden, Paxton, Kaden, Jayden.[197]

What is the most recent naming craze, you may be wondering? To figure this out, I examined twenty-first-century names in Utah by comparing the top twenty names babies were given in Utah (2001 to 2020) to the top twenty in the entire country.[198] Names that made the Utah list but not the nationwide list appear in the following table. The names in the list remind me of a wedding: something old (Eleanor), something new (Grayson), something biblical (Isaac), something Trekkie (Ryker).

Girls' Names	Boys' Names
Brooklyn	Asher
Claire	Austin
Eleanor	Brooks
Ellie	Caleb
Hazel	Carson
Ivy	Carter
Kate	Ezra
Kaylee	Gavin
Lucy	Grayson
Lydia	Hudson
Nora	Hunter
Oakley	Isaac
Paisley	Landon
Rachel	Leo
Ruby	Lincoln
Savannah	Luke
Sophie	Miles
Sydney	Owen
	Ryker
	Samuel
	Theodore
	Thomas
	Wyatt

So the most common names aren't terribly odd, but one naming trend in the state is to take an ordinary name and get creative with its spelling.[199] This is especially true for names given to baby girls: Alisha, Alivia, Bostyn,

Britni, Charlee, Emersyn, Evalyn, Izabella and Nacole. The innovation goes way beyond spellings, however. Consider these girls' names: Aaliyah, Bexley, Brexlee, Brielle, Daleyza, Haizley, Kinzlee, Nayeli, Saylor, Swayzie, Xiomara. Some imaginative boys' names you'll hear in the state are Alijah, Bodhi, Deegan, Jase, Jaxon, Jaxton, Jovanny, Kanyon, Kash, Kashton, Korver, Krew, Ledger, Raiden, Ruger, Tristyn and Zayden.

It would be nice to know whether these naming patterns are particular only to Utahns who are members of the CJCLDS, but that would be difficult to sort out. Of course, members of the CJCLDS do name their children after church leaders (Dallin, Hyrum, Spencer, Talmage), as well as give them names found in the Book of Mormon, such as Ammon, Nephi, Jared, Jarom and Alma.

One study of Utah naming practices noticed that Utah is a trendsetter for names. That is, many names that first become popular in Utah later become common in other states.[200] While certain names are more frequent in Utah than in other parts of the country, one study of Utah names concluded that "the great majority of babies born in Utah are given names which would arouse no comment in the rest of the United States.…Even some of the more creative names found in Utah probably wouldn't seem to be out of place in the rest of the country."[201]

What about surnames in the state? Smith, Johnson and Anderson top the list. Are you bored yet? What we really want to know is what surnames are more common inside the state boundaries when compared to the rest of the nation. One way to look at it is that 50 percent or more of all Americans with these last names live in Utah: Dansie, Burningham, Fowers, Francom, Buttars, Checketts. Cloward, Bangerter, Karren, Memmott, Bodily, Argyle, Willden, Thurgood, Slaugh, Behunin, Cragun, Guble, Jewkes, Esplin, Labrum and Richins. I must admit that I've never heard most of them before. That's because not all of these clans are large.

A better way to get a handle on what surnames are typically Utahn is to compare how Utah surname rankings compare with national rankings.[202] If you consider last names that differ by two hundred ranking points and then order those according to how many Utahns carry the name, you come up with surnames that often grace a Utah driver's license (see the following table). Scandinavian surnames top the list, followed by a good chunk of names from Britain, Ireland and Germany, with just a pinch of Spanish.

Jensen	Jorgensen	Wilcox	Davies	Talbot	Orton
Christensen	Bird	Cannon	Hess	Lyman	Poulsen

Larsen	Lloyd	Leavitt	Hunsaker	Shumway	Harding
Olsen	Snow	Jacobson	Norton	Bateman	Kimball
Nielsen	Barton	Giles	Strong	Lamb	Rees
Petersen	Barney	Pace	Parry	Rigby	Bullock
Nielson	Mortensen	Rowley	Wilde	Workman	Stephenson
Sorensen	Merrill	Farnsworth	Judd	Hardman	Heaton
Allred	Terry	Dalton	Baird	Jacobsen	Neilson
Rasmussen	Hardy	Robison	Maughan	Hurst	Ostler
Hatch	Warner	Wall	Hadley	Clayton	Stout
Curtis	Barlow	Fullmer	Murdock	Adamson	Cutler
Madsen	Lund	Swenson	Pratt	Winn	Atwood
Erickson	Shepherd	Atkinson	Richins	Randall	Godfrey
Andersen	Mecham	Bradshaw	Butterfield	Briggs	Vigil
Christiansen	Draper	Hancock	McBride	Parkinson	Maxfield
Barker	Sorenson	Hales	Monson	Ashby	Baxter
Bingham	Trujillo	Jolley	Child	Bradford	Andrus
Tanner	Wilkinson	Rich	Jenson	Stoddard	Durrant
Call	Gallegos	Peck	Montoya	Brinkerhoff	Earl

PONG, ATARI AND CHUCK E. CHEESE

If you look at the accompanying photo and have no idea what it is, then it is highly likely that you did not grow up in the 1970s. It's a screenshot of the world's first commercially successful video game—*Pong*. Credit for inventing the first video game actually goes to William Higinbotham, who in 1958 designed a game merely as an exhibit for visitors to Brookhaven National Laboratory; it was never patented.[203] However, Nolan Bushnell's *Pong* started the video-game craze in 1972.

Bushnell was born in Clearfield, Utah, in 1943, and his love for arcade games can be traced to his days working at Lagoon, an amusement park in Farmington, Utah. In addition to creating *Pong*, Bushnell cofounded Atari, the company that dominated the early years of video games. He later fused his video arcade games with pizza, and Chuck E. Cheese's Pizza Time Theater was born. One of Atari's first employees was Steve

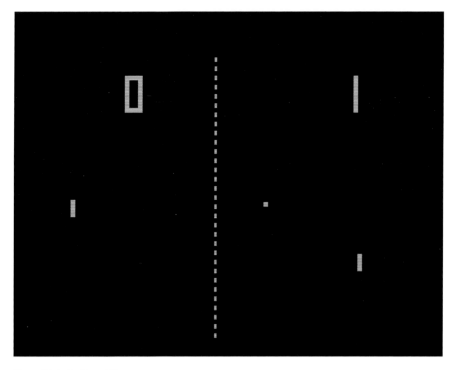

Pong. *Photo by Bumm13.*

Jobs.[204] A few years later, when Jobs was starting Apple, he asked Bushnell to invest $50,000 in the new company in exchange for a 33 percent share in it. Bushnell turned him down.

ROADOMETER

During the nineteenth century, the U.S. border kept moving west. The size of the United States doubled in 1803 when Thomas Jefferson bought the land in the Louisiana Purchase from the French. Then, in 1848, the United States took an even larger chunk of land from the Mexicans than it had bought from the French. It wasn't hard to convince people to head west. The mentality in the nineteenth century was that there was free land for the taking; you just had to kill, infect or move the Native Americans who had occupied it for generations, and it was yours. Journalist John O'Sullivan gave a name to the prevalent idea that God had ordained the U.S. borders to reach from coast to coast. He called it *manifest destiny*.[205]

Hundreds of thousands of eager settlers made their way west by wagon, handcart and horseback. Regardless of how they moved west, most people had the idea that it would be a one-way trip, that once they crossed a particular river, they'd never see it again. That mentality gave most travelers little motivation to improve the trail in any way.

The members of the CJCLDS were different in this regard. They knew that there would be a constant stream of immigrants heading west, and to aid their fellow church members in their travels, they planted crops along the trail, wrote instructions and information on dried cow skulls and built bridges and ferries. About sixty thousand people made the trek to the Salt Lake Valley on the Mormon Trail, and these trail improvements probably resulted in fewer deaths.[206]

One important thing travelers needed to know was the distance between important points along the trail. To this end, William Clayton calculated that 360 turns of his wagon wheel equaled a mile. He tired of counting the rotations all day, so along with Orson Pratt, the two designed a device made of wooden cogs and dubbed it the *roadometer*.[207] His calculations of the distances on the trail made the trip much more travel-friendly for those who

Roadometer. *Courtesy of the Utah State Historical Society.*

followed him. Although Clayton wasn't from Utah, didn't design his device in Utah and wasn't the first to devise an odometer, his roadometer deserves a place among Utahisms.

STEREO, HEARING AID

A senior citizen and a twenty-some-odd male sit next to each other on a crowded subway. While most of the passengers have their noses buried in their telephone screens, these two stare blankly ahead. The young man sports a set of ear buds whose music helps to drown out the noise of the train's wheels rumbling over the tracks. The elderly man, whose hearing has suffered the damaging effects of having worked in a factory all his life, also wears devices in his ears. Unlike the young man, in order to dampen the subway noise, he has turned his hearing aids off. What these two men have in common is that the devices they wear were both invented by Harvey Fletcher.

Fletcher was born in Provo in 1884. While Fletcher was studying for a PhD at the University of Chicago, his dissertation advisor took the research that they had carried out together, published it as his own and went on to receive the Nobel Prize in physics for it.[208] Harvey became intensely interested in acoustics, and while he was working at Bell Laboratories, he invented a way to record in stereo. That was one of the forty patents he held. He went on to invent the hearing aid, a vacuum tube–driven device. One of the first to try it was none other than Thomas Edison.[209]

STREET SYSTEM

Most cities in the United States began as farming settlements. As the population expanded, what used to be paths and trails were widened and improved into streets and roads. What this means is that a city's early street system really didn't have any kind of systematic design. This contrasts with urban developments that start with empty land and map out the streets in advance.

When the first white settlers arrived in Utah in 1847, they encountered miles of undeveloped land, a perfect scenario to lay out a complete city in advance. Brigham Young planted a post in the ground and declared that a temple would be constructed on that spot. That post became the ground zero point for mapping out the streets in Salt Lake City in a grid system using

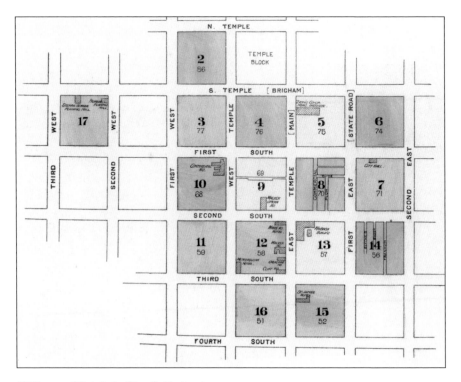

1884 map of Salt Lake City. *Public domain.*

the cardinal compass points. Settlements in the rest of the state followed this model. The way it worked was that the second block to the north of the temple plot was designated 200 North (the first block called North Temple instead of 100 North), the third block west was 300 West, the fifth block west 500 West and so on. The lack of existing buildings meant that there were no constraints on the width of the streets, so Brigham Young figured it would be nice to be able to make a U-turn in an ox-driven cart without having to back up the team. This idea is responsible for the fact that streets in Utah tend to be wider than in other states.

This system may be confusing for some who are accustomed to an address being composed of a house number followed by a street name, such as 125 South Elm Street, because in Utah, many street names are numeric as well. For example, an address of 125 East 5600 South means that a house is located fifty-six blocks south of the temple and between the first and second block east of the temple. Of course, the street can be called fifty-six hundred south, but Utahns also refer to it as 56th South, since it's the fifty-sixth block south of the temple.

TELEVISION

Philo T. Farnsworth. *Photo by Harris & Ewing.*

What do plowing fields and inventing television have in common? Quite a bit, actually. While plowing fields in 1920, fourteen-year-old Philo Farnsworth (born in Beaver, Utah) imagined transmitting light back and forth in a zigzag pattern in the same way he plowed fields. His high school teacher recalls how he sketched his idea out on the blackboard for him while still a high school student. While earlier attempts at creating television had involved moving mechanical parts, twenty-two-year-old Farnsworth gave the world a completely electronic means of capturing and re-creating televised images,[210] earning him the title of the Father of Television.

TRAFFIC LIGHT

There are about 289.5 million cars on the road in the United States,[211] and every day, more than 16,000 crashes occur.[212] How would those numbers look if it weren't for the use of the ubiquitous traffic light? Of course, traffic was first controlled by police officers who stood in the street and directed drivers in all kinds of weather. They put themselves in peril not only of bodily harm from less observant drivers but also of lung cancer from all the car exhaust that surrounded them.

The first attempt to remove traffic officers from the street was John Peake Knight's invention of a gas-lit semaphore, which was put to use in London in 1868. Unfortunately, his invention didn't catch on, but it did catch fire. Actually, it blew up after only twenty-five days in service, taking out the officer who operated it in the explosion.[213]

Traffic light. *Photo by Syafiqshahalam.*

The electric traffic light as we now know it, with green for go and red for stop, was invented in 1912 by a Salt Lake City police detective named Lester

Wire.[214] The first semaphore was enclosed in what looked like a birdhouse and was installed at the intersection of 200 South and Main Street in Salt Lake City. It was operated by a police officer sitting on the side of the road. Wire never patented the device, and other inventors added the yellow caution light and automated it. In any event, the traffic light freed police officers from the mundane task of directing traffic, and traffic safety was arguably much improved as a result.

ZAMBONI

What would you think about a person who had been inducted into the Ice Skating Institute's Hall of Fame, the United States Figure Skating Hall of Fame, the World Figure Skating Hall of Fame, the U.S. Hockey Hall of Fame and the United States Speed Skating Hall of Fame?[215] Quite the athlete, no? Well, no, Frank Zamboni was not an athlete at all.

Frank was born in Eureka, Utah, in 1901. In 1940, he and his brother opened an ice-skating rink in Paramount, California. The trouble with rinks

Zamboni. *Photo by S. Yume.*

is that the ice gets dinged up with use; it would take five men an hour and a half to lay down a new sheet of ice each day. Using old cars and a war-surplus Jeep engine, Frank built a machine that could resurface the entire rink in fifteen minutes.[216] That first machine turned into a successful international business in ice-resurfacing machines. Many a hockey enthusiast will forgo the usual trip to the snack bar during halftime because they are mesmerized by the slow-crawling Zamboni as it circles the rink, preparing the ice for the next half of the match.

NOTES

Chapter 1

1. Grant, "Trembling Giant."
2. United States Department of Agriculture, "Pando."
3. Vaux, "Dialects."
4. Bagley, *Salt Lake Cutoff.*
5. Augustyn, "Washington"; Family Search, "Oregon."
6. Vaux and Golder, *Harvard Dialect.*
7. Vaux, "Dialects."
8. Davies, *COCA, COHA, LDS, Google Books, GloWbE, iWeb, Movie, TV.*
9. Vaux and Jøhndal, *Cambridge.*

Chapter 2

10. Pullum, "Can I Help."
11. "Can I Help Who's Next?"
12. Pullum, "Can I Help."
13. Shakespeare, *Othello*, act 3, scene 3.
14. Eddington, *Utah English.*
15. Di Paolo, "Propredicate Do," 334.
16. Bigler, *Forgotten Kingdom.*
17. Isaiah 54:2.

18. *Dictionary of American Regional English*, "culinary."
19. Eddington, *Utah English.*
20. Google Books, "culinary water."
21. Di Paolo, "Propredicate Do."
22. *Dictionary of American Regional English*, "flipper crotch."
23. *Dictionary of American Regional English*, "oh for."
24. Wishydig, "(Oh) For___!"
25. Graham, "Oh For."
26. Eddington, *Utah English.*
27. Stopera and Galindo, "Do You Say."
28. Eddington, *Utah English.*
29. Christensen, "Utah's Fry Sauce."
30. Ego Ducrot, *Los sabores.*
31. Thursby, "Funeral Potatoes."
32. *Oxford English Dictionary*, "ignorant."
33. Williams and Nutter, "The Test."
34. Led Zeppelin, "Babe."
35. Williams, "Why Don't."
36. Di Paolo, "Propredicate Do."
37. Brittingham and de la Cruz, *Ancestry.*
38. Eddington, *Utah English.*
39. Abadi, "Soda."
40. Lillie, "Utah Dialect."
41. Eddington, *Utah English.*
42. *Oxford English Dictionary*, "scone."
43. Brown, "12 U.S. States."
44. Eliason, "Utah Scones."
45. *Oxford English Dictionary*, "scone."
46. *Urban Dictionary*, "sluff."
47. *Dictionary of American Regional English*, "slough."
48. Vaux, "Dialects."
49. Bert Vaux (personal communication) indicated that the map for *sluff* in the survey was incorrect due to a computer glitch, and he furnished me with a corrected version that this figure is based on.
50. Eddington, *Utah English.*
51. Lillie, "Utah Dialect."
52. Eddington, *Utah English.*
53. Canham, "Utah Effect."
54. Harrison, "Crash Course."

55. Carey, "Sweary Maps."

56. Fretts, Tucker, Wolk and Shaw, *Survivor*.

Chapter 3

57. Judges 12:5–6.

58. Labov, Ash and Boberg, *Atlas*.

59. Eckert, "Ethnolects."

60. Hickey, "Mergers"; Thomas, "Acoustic Analysis."

61. Barrett, "American Glottalization."

62. Labov, Ash and Boberg, *Atlas*.

63. Savage, "How We Feel."

64. Eddington, *Utah English*.

65. Twain, *Adventures*, 108.

66. Vaux and Golder, *Harvard Dialect*.

67. Lillie, "Utah Dialect."

68. *Merriam Webster*, "creek."

69. Eddington, *Utah English*.

70. Labov, Ash and Boberg, *Atlas*.

71. Vaux and Golder, *Harvard Dialect*.

72. Pardoe, "Some Studies."

73. Bowie, "Early Development."

74. Salvesen, "Tubes of Saliva."

75. Bowie, "Early Development"; Bowie, "Early Trends."

76. Helquist, "Phonological Variable"; Lillie, "Utah Dialect."

77. Cook, "Language Change"; Sarver, "Transferability"; Savage, "How We Feel."

78. Baker, Eddington and Nay. "Dialect Identification."

79. Lillie, "Utah Dialect."

80. Sarver, "Transferability."

81. Baker and Bowie, "Religious Affiliation."

82. Davies, *GloWbE*.

83. Gordon, "The West"; Labov, Yaeger and Steiner, "Quantitative"; Sledd, "Canterbury Tell."

84. Giauque and Richards, "Would-Be Robbers."

85. Baker, Eddington and Nay. "Dialect Identification."

86. Labov, Ash and Boberg, *Atlas*.

87. Lillie, "Utah Dialect."

88. Eddington, *Utah English.*

89. Savage, "How We Feel."

90. Kerswill, "Dialect Levelling."

91. Labov, Ash and Boberg, *Atlas.*

92. Bowie, "Early Trends."

93. Di Paolo, "Hypercorrection."

94. Sarver, "Transferability."

95. Baker-Smemoe and Bowie, "Linguistic Behavior."

96. Di Paolo, "Hypercorrection."

97. Labov, Ash and Boberg, *Atlas.*

98. Eckert, "Ethnolects."

99. Clarke, Elms and Youssef, "Third Dialect."

100. Lillie, "Utah Dialect."

101. Eddington, *Utah English.*

102. Ibid.

103. *Merriam Webster*, "measure."

104. Savage, "How We Feel."

105. Eddington, *Utah English.*

106. Bowie, "Early Trends."

107. Morkel, "Tracing."

108. Sykes, "Sociophonetic Study."

109. Sarver, "Transferability."

110. Baker-Smemoe and Bowie, "Linguistic Behavior."

111. *Oxford English Dictionary*, "acrost."

112. Language Log, "acrosst."

113. Savage, "How We Feel."

114. Stanley and Vanderniet, "Consonantal Variation."

115. Savage, "How We Feel."

116. Eddington, *Utah English.*

117. Vaux and Golder, *Harvard Dialect.*

118. Vaux, "Dialects."

119. Eddington, *Utah English.*

120. Labov, Ash and Boberg, *Atlas*; Lillie, "Utah Dialect."

121. Eddington, *Utah English*; Baker-Smemoe and Bowie, "Linguistic Behavior."

122. Eddington, *Utah English.*

123. Vaux and Golder, *Harvard Dialect.*

124. Di Paolo and Faber, "Phonation Differences"; Faber and Di Paolo, "Discriminability."

125. Vaux and Golder, *Harvard Dialect*.
126. Lillie, "Utah Dialect."
127. Sarver, "Transferability."
128. Eddington, *Utah English*.
129. Lillie, "Utah Dialect."
130. *Cambridge Dictionary*, "tour."
131. *Oxford Learner's Dictionaries*, "tour."
132. Eddington, *Utah English*.
133. Eddington and Savage, "Where Are."
134. Stanley and Vanderniet, "Consonantal Variation."
135. Savage, "How We Feel."
136. Eddington and Brown, "Production."
137. Davidson et al., "The Link."
138. Eddington and Brown, "Production."

Chapter 4

139. Van Cott, *Utah Place Names*.
140. Todt, "Beaver College."
141. Benson, "About Utah."
142. Van Cott, *Utah Place Names*, 36.
143. *Los Angeles Times*, "Tank Rampage."
144. Van Cott, *Utah Place Names*, 62.
145. Ibid., 118.
146. Ibid., 119.
147. Ibid., 183.
148. *Deseret News*, "Hooper."
149. Word Reference, "hooper."
150. Washington County Historical Society, "Hurricane Canal."
151. Daughters of Utah Pioneers, historic marker.
152. *Cambridge Dictionary*, "hurricane."
153. DeMille, *Portraits*.
154. Brown, "12 U.S. States."
155. Hall, "History."
156. Ibid.
157. Dilts, *1860*.
158. Arave, "Navel Myth."
159. Van Cott, *Utah Place Names*, 225.
160. Dean and Headrick, "Most-Likely Spots."

161. Associated Press, "Mantua."
162. Van Cott, *Utah Place Names*, 331.
163. Bright, *Native American*.
164. Van Cott, *Utah Place Names*, 208.
165. Ibid., 331.
166. Santaquin, "Santaquin History."
167. Allred, *Icelanders*.
168. Bolton et al., "Pageant."
169. Scribner, "Does Utah."
170. United States Department of Agriculture, "American Fork."
171. Hampl et al., "Scourge."
172. Van Cott, *Utah Place Names*. The towns of St. David, Arizona, and St. Charles, Idaho, were also named in honor of church leaders.
173. *Britannica*, "Timpanogos Cave."
174. Farmer, *Zion's Mount*.
175. Bolton et al., "Pageant."
176. Ibid.
177. Tripp, "Tooele—What."
178. eReference Desk. "Utah State."
179. Brigham Young High School History, "Y."
180. Lafazan, "The 'U.'"

Chapter 5

181. Arrington, *Great Basin*.
182. Bradley, *ZCMI*.
183. Arrington, *Great Basin*.
184. Bradley, *ZCMI*.
185. Graña, *Pioneer*.
186. Washington County Historical Society, "Text."
187. Kennedy and Morrison, "Frisbee."
188. Pearce, "Harland Sanders."
189. Phillips, "50 Years."
190. Comen, "These 9 States."
191. Wikipedia, "Alcohol Beverage Control."
192. Botelho, "NTSB Calls For."
193. Stephenson, "13 Liquor Facts."
194. Ibid.

195. Clark, "Utah Name."
196. Evans, "Naming."
197. Ibid.
198. *Social Security*, "Beyond the Top."
199. *Daily Herald*, "25."
200. Evans, "Naming."
201. Ibid.
202. *Forebears*, Most Common,"
203. APS News, "Physics History."
204. Isaacson, *Steve Jobs*.
205. O'Sullivan, "Manifest Destiny."
206. Pappas, "Going West."
207. Bellis, "Odometer."
208. Fletcher, "My Work."
209. Curtis, "Utah Inventions."
210. Schatzkin, *Television*.
211. Hedges and Company, "Vehicle Registrations."
212. *Wandering RV*, "Car Accident."
213. *BBC Home*, "Traffic Lights."
214. Crofts, "Utah Inventions."
215. Zamboni, "Awards/Recognition."
216. Folkart, "Frank Zamboni."

BIBLIOGRAPHY

Abadi, Mark. "'Soda' 'Pop,' or 'Coke': More Than 400,000 Americans Weighed In, and a Map of Their Answers Is Exactly What You'd Expect." *Business Insider*, October 6, 2018. www.businessinsider.in/soda-pop-or-coke-more-than-400000-americans-weighed-in-and-a-map-of-their-answers-is-exactly-what-youd-expect/articleshow/66074186.cms.

Allred, LaNora. *The Icelanders of Utah*. Spanish Fork: Icelandic Association of Utah, 1990.

America's Health Rankings. "Annual Report 2019." americashealthrankings.org/app/uploads/ahr_2019annualreport.pdf.

AP News. "This Month in Physics History. October 1958: Physicist Invents First Video Game." *APS News* 17, no. 9 (2008). www.aps.org/publications/apsnews/200810/physicshistory.cfm.

Arave, Lynn. "Levan, Utah: Sinkng [*sic*] the Navel Myth." *The Mystery of Utah History*, May 19, 2017. mysteryofutahhistory.blogspot.com/2017/05/levan-utah-sinkng-navel-myth.html.

Arrington, Leonard J. *Great Basin Kingdom: Economic History of the Latter-Day Saints*. Lincoln: University of Nebraska Press, 1958.

Associated Press. "Mantua Boasts Mean Speed Trap." *Deseret News*, March 10, 1998. www.deseret.com/1998/3/10/19367995/mantua-boasts-mean-speed-trap.

Augustyn, Adam. "Washington State, United States." *Encyclopædia Britannica*. www.britannica.com/place/Washington-state.

Bagley, W. *S.J. Hensley's Salt Lake Cutoff*. Salt Lake City: Oregon-California Trails Association, Utah Crossroads Chapter, 1992.

Baker, Wendy, and David Bowie. "Religious Affiliation as a Correlate of Linguistic Behavior." *University of Pennsylvania Working Papers in Linguistics* 15, no. 2 (2010): 2.

Baker, Wendy, David Eddington and Lyndsey Nay. "Dialect Identification: The Effects of Region of Origin and Amount of Experience." *American Speech* 84, no. 1 (2009): 48–71.

Baker-Smemoe, Wendy, and David Bowie. "Linguistic Behavior and Religious Activity." *Language and Communication* 42 (2015): 116–24.

Barrett, Grant. "American Glottalization." A Way with Words. January 30, 2017. www.waywordradio.org/american-glottalization/

BBC Home. "The Man Who Gave Us Traffic Lights." November 13, 2014. www.bbc.co.uk/nottingham/content/articles/2009/07/16/john_peake_knight_traffic_lights_feature.shtml.

Bellis, Mary. "The History of the Odometer." *Thought Co.*, April 6, 2019www.thoughtco.com/history-of-odometers-4074178.

Benson, Lee. "About Utah: Beaver's Water Is Worth a Stop." *Deseret News*, November 18, 2009. www.deseret.com/2009/11/18/20353496/about-utah-beaver-s-water-is-worth-a-stop.

Bigler, David L. *Forgotten Kingdom: The Mormon Theocracy in the American West, 1847–1896.* Logan: Utah State University Press, 1998.

Bolton, Herbert E., Arlington R. Mortensen and Bernardo Miera y Pacheco. "Pageant in the Wilderness: The Story of the Escalante Expedition to the Interior Basin, 1776: Including the Diary and Itinerary of Father Escalante Translated and Annotated." *Utah Historical Quarterly* 18, no. 1/4 (1950): vii–265.

Botelho, Greg, "NTSB Calls for Lowering Blood Alcohol Limit, but Is That the Answer?" *CNN*, February 16, 2016. www.cnn.com/2016/02/05/us/drunken-driving-blood-alcohol-limit/index.html.

Bowie, David. "Early Development of the Card-Cord Merger in Utah." *American Speech* 78, no. 1 (2003): 31–51.

———. "Early Trends in a Newly Developing Variety of English." *Dialectologia: Revista Electrònica* 8 (2012): 27–47.

Bradley, Martha Sonntag. *ZCMI: America's First Department Store.* Salt Lake City: ZCMI, 1991.

Brigham Young High School History. "Y on the Mountainside." www.byhigh.org/History/Ymountain/Yletter.html.

Bright, William. *Native American Place Names of the United States.* Norman: University of Oklahoma Press, 2004.

Britannica. "Timpanogos Cave National Monument." www.britannica.com/ place/Timpanogos-Cave-National-Monument.

Brittingham, Angela, and Patricia de la Cruz. *Ancestry: 2000*. Vol. 3. U.S. Department of Commerce, Economics and Statistics Administration: U.S. Census Bureau, 2004.

Brown, Lawrence. "12 U.S. States with the Highest Concentration of English Ancestry." Updated February 20, 2014. www.lostinthepond. com/2014/02/12-us-states-with-highest-concentration.html.

Cambridge Dictionary, s.v. "hurricane." dictionary.cambridge.org/us/ pronunciation/english/hurricane.

Canham, Matt. "The Utah Effect: The $%&* People Tweet by State." *Salt Lake Tribune*, July 30, 2015. archive.sltrib.com/article. php?id=2762317anditype=CMSID.

"Can I Help Who's Next?" *Separated by a Common Language*. Updated October 19, 2007. separatedbyacommonlanguage.blogspot. com/2007/10/can-i-help-whos-next.html.

Carey, Stan. "Sweary Maps 2: Swear Harder." *Strong Language*, March 22, 2016. stronglang.wordpress.com/2016/03/22/sweary-maps-2-swear-harder.

Christensen, Michael P. "Utah's Fry Sauce." In *This Is the Plate: Utah Food Traditions*, edited by Carol A. Edison, Eric A. Eliason and Lynne S. McNeill, 36–44. Salt Lake City: University of Utah Press, 2020.

Clark, Cari Bilyeu. "What's in a Utah Name?" *The Original Utah Baby Namer*, June 5, 2017. utahbabynamer.blogspot.com/2017/06/front-page. html.

Clarke, Sandra, Ford Elms and Amani Youssef. "The Third Dialect of English: Some Canadian Evidence." *Language Variation and Change* 7, no. 2 (1995): 209–28.

Comen, Evan. "These 9 States Still Have Dry Counties." *24/7 Wall Street*. December 12, 2019. 247wallst.com/special-report/2019/12/12/states-that-still-have-dry-counties.

Cook, Stanley J. "Language Change and the Emergence of an Urban Dialect in Utah." PhD diss., University of Utah, 1969.

Crofts, Natalie. "Utah Inventions: The World's 1ˢᵗ Electric Traffic Light." *KSL.com*, August 12, 2015. www.ksl.com/article/35930882.

Curtis, Ryan D. "Utah Inventions: Harvey Fletcher, the Father of Stereophonic Sound." *KSL.com*. www.ksl.com/article/36745114/utah-inventions-harvey-fletcher-the-father-of-stereophonic-sound.

Daily Herald. "25 of the Most Unique Names in Utah County." March 3, 2020. www.heraldextra.com/news/local/of-the-most-unique-names-in-utah-valley/collection_f0d3f110-c84f-565d-af2c-bcee5ee2940d.html#1.

Daughters of Utah Pioneers. Historic marker. September 25, 1931. Located in Heritage Park, 35 West State Street, Hurricane, Utah.

Davidson, Lisa, Shmico Orosco and Sheng-Fu Wang. "The Link between Syllabic Nasals and Glottal Stops in American English." *Laboratory Phonology: Journal of the Association for Laboratory Phonology* 12, no. 1 (2021).

Davies, Mark. *The Corpus of Contemporary American English (COCA): 560 Million Words, 1990–present.* 2005. corpus.byu.edu/coca.

———. *Corpus of Global Web-Based English: 1.9 Billion Words from Speakers in 20 Countries (GloWbE).* 2013. corpus.byu.edu/glowbe.

———. *The Corpus of Historical American English (COHA): 400 Million Words, 1810–2009.* 2010. corpus.byu.edu/coha.

———. *The 14 Billion Word iWeb Corpus. 2018–.* 2018. corpus.byu.edu/iWeb.

———. *Google Books Corpus (Based on Google Books n-grams), 2011–.* 2011. googlebooks.byu.edu.

———. LDS General Conference Corpus. 2011. www.lds-general-conference.org.

———. *The Movie Corpus: 200 Million Words, 1930–2018.* 2019. corpus.byu.edu/movies.

———. *The TV Corpus: 325 Million Words, 1950–2018.* 2019. corpus.byu.edu/tv.

Dean, Tania, and Mike Headrick. "Most-Likely Spots in Utah for Speeding Tickets." *Deseret News*, February 26, 2019. www.ksl.com/article/46499406/most-likely-spots-in-utah-for-speeding-tickets.

DeMille, Janice Force. *Portraits of the Hurricane Pioneers.* N.p.: Homestead Publishers, 1976.

Deseret News. "Hooper: How Do You Say Hooper?" October 21, 2007. www.deseret.com/2007/10/21/20048475/hooper-how-do-you-say-hooper.

Dictionary of American Regional English. s.v. "culinary water." search.lib.byu.edu/byu/search?=dictionary+of+american+regional+english.

———. s.v. "flipper crotch." www.daredictionary.com/view/dare/ID_00064851.

———. s.v. "oh for." www.daredictionary.com/view/dare/ID_00041127.

———. s.v. "slough." search.lib.byu.edu/byu/search?q=dictionary+of+american+regional+english.

Dilts, Bryan Lee, ed. *1860 District of Columbia Census Index: Heads of Households and Other Surnames in Households Index.* Salt Lake City, UT: Index, 1983.

Di Paolo, Marianna. "Hypercorrection in Response to the Apparent Merger of (ɔ) and (ɑ) in Utah English." *Language and Communication* 12, nos. 3–4 (1992): 267–92.

———. "Propredicate Do in the English of the Intermountain West." *American Speech* 68, no. 4 (1993): 339–56.

Di Paolo, Marianna, and Alice Faber. "Phonation Differences and the Phonetic Content of the Tense-Lax Contrast in Utah English." *Language Variation and Change* 2, no. 2 (1990): 155–204.

Eckert, Penelope. "Where Do Ethnolects Stop?" *International Journal of Bilingualism* 12, nos. 1–2 (2008): 25–42.

Eddington, David. *Utah English.* Salt Lake City: University of Utah Press, (2022).

Eddington, David Ellingson, and Earl Kjar Brown. "A Production and Perception Study of /t/ Glottalization and Oral Releases Following Glottals in the United States." *American Speech*, (forthcoming).

Eddington, David, and Matthew Savage. "Where Are the Moun[ʔə]ns in Utah?" *American Speech* 87 (2012): 336–49.

Ego Ducrot, Victor. *Los sabores de la patria: Las intrigas de la historia argentina contadas desde la mesa y la cocina.* Buenos Aires: Grupo Editorial Norma, 1998.

Eliason, Eric A. "Utah Scones." In *This Is the Plate: Utah Food Traditions*, edited by Carol A. Edison, Eric A. Eliason and Lynne S. McNeill, 52–55. Salt Lake City: University of Utah Press, 2020.

Evans, Cleveland K. "Contemporary Latter-day Saint Naming." In "Names, Identity, and Belief: Perspectives on Latter-day Saint Names and Naming," edited by Dallin D. Oaks, Paul Baltes and Kent Minson. Unpublished manuscript, Brigham Young University, 2021.

Faber, Alice, and Marianna Di Paolo. "The Discriminability of Nearly Merged Sounds." *Language Variation and Change* 78 (1995): 35–78.

Family Search. "Oregon Emigration and Immigration." www.familysearch.org/wiki/en/Oregon_Emigration_and_Immigration#:~:text=1811%2C%20John%20Jacob%20Astor%2C%C%20an,eastern%20states%2C%20Canada%20and%20Russia.

Farmer, Jared. *On Zion's Mount: Mormons, Indians, and the American Landscape.* Cambridge, MA: Harvard University Press, 2008.

Fletcher, Harvey. "My Work with Millikan on the Oil-Drop Experiment." *Physics Today* (June 1982): 43–47.

Folkart, Burt A. "Obituaries: Frank Zamboni: The Man Behind That Odd Machine." *Los Angeles Times*, July 28, 1988. www.latimes.com/archives/la-xpm-1988-07-29-mn-8143-story.html.

Forebears. "Most Common Last Names in Utah." forebears.io/united-states/utah/surnames.

Fretts, Bruce, Ken Tucker, Josh Wolk and Jessica Shaw. "*Survivor: Marquesas.*" *Entertainment Weekly*, updated May 17, 2002. ew.com/article/2002/05/17/survivor-marquesas.

Galdamez, Misael, Charlotte Kesteven and Aaron Melaas. "Best Performing Cities 2021: Foundations for Growth and Recovery." Milken Institute, 2021. milkeninstitute.org/reports/best-performing-cities-2021.

George, Sarah, and Catherine Choi. "Worst Drivers by State in 2021." *Finder*, March 5, 2021. www.finder.com/worst-drivers-by-state.

Giauque, Marc, and Mary Richards. "Would-Be Robbers Walk Away Empty-Handed," *KSL.com*, April 11, 2008. www.ksl.com/article/3058039.

Google Books, s.v. "culinary water." books.google.com.

Gordon, Matthew. "The West and Midwest: Phonology." In *Varieties of English 2: The Americas and the Caribbean*, edited by Edgar W. Schneider, 129–42. Berlin: Mouton de Gruyter, 2008.

Graham, Janna. "'Oh For' as a Scandinavian-Influenced Linguistic Feature of Minnesota and Utah." Paper presented at the 60th Annual RMMLA Convention, Tucson, AZ, October 12–14, 2006.

Graña, Mari. *Pioneer, Polygamist, Politician: The Life of Dr. Martha Hughes Cannon.* Guilford, CT: Twodot, 2009.

Grant, Michael C. "The Trembling Giant." *Discover* 14 (1993): 82–89.

Hall, Victor. "The History of La Verkin." cdn.sqhk.co/laverkincity/bFijXie/VictorHallEssay.pdf.

Hampl, Jeffrey S. "Scourge of Black-Leg (Scurvy) on the Mormon Train." *Nutrition* 17, no. 5 (2001): 416–18.

Harrison, Mette Ivie. "A Crash Course on Mormon Cursing." *Huffpost*, updated October 14, 2016. www.huffpost.com/entry/mormon-cursing_b_8281022.

Hedges and Company. "U.S. Vehicle Registrations Statistics." hedgescompany.com/automotive-market-research-statistics/auto-mailing-lists-and-marketing.

Helquist, Val J. "A Study of One Phonological Variable in Urban and Rural Utah." PhD diss., University of Utah, 1970.

Hickey, Raymond. "Mergers, Near-Mergers, and Phonological Interpretation." *New Perspectives on English Historical Linguistics: Selected Papers from 12 ICEHL, Glasgow, 21–26 August 2002. Volume II: Lexis and Transmission* 252 (2004): 125.

Ho, Erica. "How Foul-Mouthed Is America?: Profanity and Swears Mapped Out." *Time*, January 25, 2011. newsfeed.time.com/2011/01/25/americans-are-dirty-profanity-and-swears-mapped-out.

Isaacson, Walter. *Steve Jobs.* New York: Simon and Schuster, 2011.

Kennedy, Phil, and Fred Morrison. "The History of the Frisbee." www.flatflip.com/downloads/A%20Short%20History%20of%20the%20Frisbee.pdf.

Kerswill, Paul. "Dialect Levelling and Geographical Diffusion in British English." In *Social Dialectology: In Honour of Peter Trudgill*, edited by David Britain and Jenny Cheshire, 223–43. Amsterdam: John Benjamins, n.d.

Labov, William, Sharon Ash and Charles Boberg. *The Atlas of North American English: Phonetics, Phonology and Sound Change.* Berlin/New York: Walter de Gruyter, 2006.

Labov, William, Malcah Yaeger and Richard Steiner. *A Quantitative Study of Sound Change in Progress.* Philadelphia: U.S. Regional Survey, 1972.

Lafazan, Alison. "The 'U' on the Mountain." *Utah Stories*, December 30, 2017. utahstories.com/2017/12/the-u-on-the-mountain.

Language Log. "Acrosst." July 28, 2010. languagelog.ldc.upenn.edu/nll/?p=2495.

Led Zeppelin. "Babe I'm Gonna Leave You." Track 2 on *Led Zeppelin* LP, originally released in 1969.

Lillie, Diane DeFord. "The Utah Dialect Survey." Master's thesis, Brigham Young University, 1998.

Los Angeles Times. "Tank Rampage in San Diego Ends Plumber's Troubled Life." May 19, 1995. www.sun-sentinel.com/news/fl-xpm-1995-05-19-9505190016-story.html.

Merriam Webster. s.v. "creek." www.merriam-webster.com/dictionary/creek.
———. s.v. "measure." www.merriam-webster.com/dictionary/measure.

Morkel, Wendy McCollum. "Tracing a Sound Pattern: /Ay/ Monophthongization in Utah English." Master's thesis, Brigham Young University, 2003.

O'Sullivan, John L. "Manifest Destiny." In *1845: Manifest Destiny and the Imperialism Question*, edited by Châties L. Sanford, 26–32. New York: John Wiley and Sons, 1974.

Oxford English Dictionary. s.v. "acrost." www-oed-com.erl.lib.byu.edu/view/
Entry/1866?redirectedFrom=acrost#eid.

———. s.v. "ignorant." www-oed-com.erl.lib.byu.edu/view/Entry/91234?
redirectedFrom=ignorant#eid.

———. s.v. "scone." www-oed-com.erl.lib.byu.edu/view/Entry/172944?rs
key=y5wiWIandresult=1#eid.

Oxford Learner's Dictionaries. s.v. "tour." www.oxfordlearnersdictionaries.com/
us/definition/english/tour_1?q=tour.

Pappas, Stephanie. "Going West Wasn't So Deadly for Early Mormon
Pioneers." *Live Science,* July 16, 2014. www.livescience.com/46834-
mormon-pioneers-mortality-rate.html.

Pardoe, T. Earle. "Some Studies of Rocky Mountain Dialects." *Quarterly
Journal of Speech* 21, no. 3 (1935): 348–55.

Pearce, John, ed. "Harland Sanders: The Man Who Would Be Colonel."
In *The Human Tradition in the New South*, edited by J.C. Klotter, 129–56.
Lanham, MD: Rowman and Littlefield Publishers, 2005.

Phillips, Valerie. "50 Years of Finger-Lickin' Chicken." *Deseret News,* July
30, 2002. www.deseret.com/2002/7/30/19668918/50-years-of-finger-
lickin-chicken.

Pullum, Geoffrey. "Can I Help Who's Next." *Language Log*, updated
December 4, 2005. itre.cis.upenn.edu/~myl/languagelog/
archives/002690.html.

Salvesen, Anis. "What 770,000 Tubes of Saliva Reveal About America."
Ancestry, February 8, 2017. blogs.ancestry.com/cm/what-770000-tubes-
of-saliva-reveal-about-america.

Santaquin. "Santaqin History." www.santaquin.org/our_community/
santaquin_history.

Sarver, Daniel A. "The Transferability of Utah English Characteristics:
Second Dialect (D2) Acquisition in Utah." Honors thesis, Brigham
Young University, 2004.

Savage, David Matthew. "How We Feel about How We Talk: A Language
Attitude Survey of Utah English." Master's thesis, Brigham Young
University, 2014.

Schatzkin, Paul. *The Boy Who Invented Television: A Story of Inspiration,
Persistence, and Quiet Passion.* Silver Spring, MD: TeamCom Books, 2002.

Scribner, Herb. "Does Utah Really Host the World's Largest Holi Festival?"
Deseret News, March 15, 2017. www.deseret.com/2017/3/15/20608302/
does-utah-really-host-the-world-s-largest-holi-festival.

Shakespeare, William. *Othello: The Moor of Venice*. Edited by Mark Mussari. New York: Marshall Cavendish Benchmark, 2010.

Sledd, J. "A Canterbury Tell." *American Speech* 62 (1987) 185–86.

Social Security. "Beyond the Top 1000 Names." www.ssa.gov/oact/babynames/limits.html.

Stanley, Joseph A., and Kyle Vanderniet. "Consonantal Variation in Utah English: What El[t]se Is Happening[k]?" Paper presented at the 4[th] Annual Linguistics Conference, University of Georgia, Athens, GA, 2019.

Stephenson, Kathy. "13 Liquor Facts Every Utahn Should Know—Whether You Drink or Not." *Salt Lake Tribune*, September 27, 2021. www.sltrib.com/artsliving/food/2021/09/19/liquor-facts-every-utahn.

Stopera, Matt, and Brian Galindo. "Do You Say These Things Like a Normal Person?" *Buzzfeed*, January 18, 2017. www.buzzfeed.com/mjs538/why-are-they-called-tennis-shoes-if-youre-not-even-playing-t.

Sykes, Robert D. "A Sociophonetic Study of (aɪ) in Utah English." Master's thesis, University of Utah, 2010.

Thomas, Erik R. "An Acoustic Analysis of Vowel Variation in New World English." Durham, NC: Duke University Press, 2001.

Thursby, Jacqueline S. "Funeral Potatoes in Utah." In *This Is the Plate: Utah Food Traditions*, edited by Carol A. Edison, Eric A. Eliason and Lynne S. McNeill, 45–51. Salt Lake City: University of Utah Press, 2020.

Todt, Ron. "Beaver College Announces New Name." *ABC News*, January 7, 2006. abcnews.go.com/US/story?id=94962&page=1.

Tripp, George. "Tooele—What Is the Name's Origin?" *Utah Historical Quarterly* 57 (1989): 273–76.

TRUiC. "Best States to Start a Business." August 27, 2021. howtostartanllc.com/start-a-business/best-states-to-start-a-business.

Twain, Mark. *Adventures of Huckleberry Finn*. San Jose, CA: New Millenium Library, 2001.

United States Department of Agriculture. "Pando." www.fs.usda.gov/detail/fishlake/home/?cid=STELPRDB5393641.

———. "Place Names on the Uinta National Forest, American Fork." www.fs.usda.gov/detail/uwcnf/learning/history-culture/?cid=fsem_035514.

Urban Dictionary. s.v. "sluff." www.urbandictionary.com/define.php?term=sluff.

Van Cott, John W. *Utah Place Names: A Comprehensive Guide to the Origins of Geographic Names: A Compilation*. Salt Lake City: University of Utah Press, 1990.

Vaux, Bert. "Dialects of American English Survey." 2018. www.dialectsofenglish.com.

Vaux, Bert, and Marius L. Jøhndal. *Cambridge Online Survey of World Englishes*. 2009. survey.johndal.com/results/.

Vaux, Bert, and Scott Golder. *The Harvard Dialect Survey.* Cambridge, MA: Harvard University Linguistics Department, 2003. dialect.redlog.net.

Washington County Historical Society. "The Hurricane Canal." wchsutah.org/water/hurricane-canal.php.

———. "Text of the Edmunds-Tucker Act of 1887." wchsutah.org/laws/edmunds-tucker-act1.php.

Williams, Gary, and Alice Nutter. "The Test." November 9, 2010. Jimmy McGovern, executive producer, *Moving on.* BBC One.

Williams, Hank. "Why Don't You Love Me?" Side A. MGM Records. Originally released in 1950.

Wishydig. "(Oh) For ___!" Updated June 26, 2009. wishydig.blogspot.com/2009/06/oh-for.html.

Word Reference. "Hooper." www.wordreference.com/definition/hooper.

Zamboni. "Awards/Recognition." zamboni.com/about/zamboni-archives/awardsrecognition.

ABOUT THE AUTHOR

 avid Ellingson Eddington is a native Utahn. He was born in Murray, raised in Holladay and presently resides with the love of his life in Woodland Hills in a log home at six thousand feet, where they are often visited by their fourteen grandchildren. He is a professor of linguistics at Brigham Young University, where, in addition to Utah dialect, he specializes in the Spanish language.

Visit us at
www.historypress.com